Beautiful SOFTWARE

by
Chuck
Connell

ISBN: 1456438786
ISBN-13: 9781456438784

Dedication

To my father, for everything he gave me in the beginning; to my wife and children, for everything they give me now; and to my friends and teachers, for help and fun throughout.

Acknowledgements

Earlier versions of this work appeared in Dr. Dobbs Journal (ddj.com), Developer.com, Slashdot.com, IBM Developer Network (ibm.com/developerworks), IPWatchdog.com, and LinuxToday.com. These publishers and editors gave me a forum to develop a writing career and, where needed, gave me permission to reuse the articles in this book.

Eric Raymond kindly allowed me to republish our spirited exchange about the management of open source projects. Steve Homer at Boston University and Judy Stafford at Tufts helped with interesting discussions that sparked some of these ideas.

Phil Margolis suggested many improvements and spurred me, by example, to improve my writing. My wife and son read the whole manuscript and pointed out some embarrassing errors.

I stole a chapter title from Alice Childress.

Table of Contents

Introduction

Software quality matters. Software runs all our banking operations, air traffic control, stock markets, car engines, train and subway switching, military weapons, global navigation, medical equipment, personal information privacy, and many other facets of our lives. Good software helps all of these things run smoothly; bad software has the potential to hurt or even kill people.

There are vast differences between high-quality software and inferior software. Good software is easier to understand, is easier to modify, and is usually shorter and simpler. It also has fewer bugs, is easier to fix when a bug is found, and often runs faster. Some software products are just better than others.

But what, exactly, distinguishes good software from bad software? Expert programmers know good software when they see it, and they are likely to produce it themselves. What do they see in the better software that makes it better? And how do they write it? Are there universal principles of good software design, that all high-quality examples share, and which are absent from poor software? If so, what are these principles? How do we go about writing software so it is likely to turn out well?

I began work in the computer field at Data General in 1980. Since then, I have worked at other exciting companies, large and small, and have studied computer science and taught it. Throughout these three decades – from my first project at DG to the most recent class I taught – I have been intrigued by the questions above. This book is an attempt to answer some of them.

Each chapter was originally published as a separate essay. For this book, I revised some of the text and rearranged the essays into three related groups: software design, management of software projects, and the field of software engineering.

SOFTWARE
DESIGN

Beautiful Software

Most software design is lousy. Most software is so bad, in fact, that if it were a bridge, no one in his or her right mind would walk across it. If it were a house, we would be afraid to enter it. The only reason we (software engineers) get away with this scam is that the general public cannot see inside of software systems. If software design were as visible as a bridge or house, we would be hiding our heads in shame.

We would not accept a new house with sloping floors, holes in the ceilings, nails sticking out of the walls, and an outrageous price – even if it minimally met basic needs. We would not be content with the explanation, "Well, it has a front door, which usually opens. You can find your way to the kitchen, but watch out for the nails.

The holes in the ceiling don't really leak. And sure it ran 300% over budget, but houses often do."

Rather than crooked floors, the software manifestations of poor design are redundancy, unnecessary performance bottlenecks, intertwined bugs that cannot be fixed, impenetrable code, and other ills. Unfortunately, we often accept software in just such a state. Regularly, companies release code like this to external and internal customers. And customers accept delivery. Businesses pay billions of dollars per year for this kind of software during mergers and acquisitions.

This article is a challenge to engineers, managers, executives, and software users (which is everyone) to raise our standards about software. We should expect the same level of quality and performance in software as we demand in physical construction. Instead of trying to create software that works in a minimal sense, we should be creating software that has internal beauty. Beautiful programs work better, cost less, match user needs, have fewer bugs, run faster, are easier to fix, and have a longer life span. Raising our standards for software is not a luxury to be reserved for programmers with extra time on their hands. Creating aesthetically pleasing software is crucial to creating better and less expensive software – in fact, they are one and the same endeavor.

Software aesthetics is a qualitative judgment, but, like physical architecture, it includes some general principles. All beautiful software has the following properties.

- Cooperation
- Appropriate form
- System minimality
- Component singularity
- Functional locality
- Readability
- Simplicity

Cooperation

Just as a building should be designed to blend with and enhance its site, software should work well with its surroundings. The site for a building is the slope of its land, its orientation to the sun, its local weather, other buildings nearby, etc. The "site" for a software system is its computer hardware, the operating system, any middleware (such as database or security systems), other software applications on the computer, and the style of the intended users.

Examples of software systems that cooperate with their environment include:

- A pocketsize electronic appointment book that works within the limitations of its small display screen, and still manages to display information clearly.

- An income-tax filing system that allows people to submit returns through the Internet, because many users already have Internet access.

- A reading tutorial for second-grade students that runs quickly on older computers, since schools are likely to have old computers rather than the latest technology.

- A more technical example is a large-scale document management system I worked on. The software architect cleverly designed the low-level storage and retrieval methods to take into account the operating properties of the computer's disk controller, so the whole system worked as efficiently as possible.

In all of these cases, the software is working in cooperation with its environment – just as a well-designed building works in harmony with its site.

Appropriate Form

The internal design of a software system should reflect and create its external functions. Beautiful buildings merge form and function, and good (beautiful) software does the same.

Why does this matter though? As long as a software system works correctly, does it matter which internal design achieves that end? It does matter. An internal structure that acknowledges the external features is more likely to create those features correctly. A software form that follows the software's function also is likely to be simpler, since the external features arise from the internal design, rather than being forced on top of the design. A software system whose form does not mirror its function will forever be difficult to debug, will have more bugs, will be difficult to extend and modify, and will likely perform its core functions poorly.

Since we cannot see or touch software, it is sometimes difficult to judge whether a software system's form matches its function. All software has a definite form, however. Consider an accounting system. Business accounting consists of several well-defined operations: purchasing, billing, payroll, general ledger, etc. To a large extent these functions are separate, but there is some overlap among them. A software system for business accounting should reflect these logical accounting operations in its internal design. There should be clearly defined parts of the software for purchasing, billing, payroll, etc. There also should be clear overlap in the software where the logical operations overlap. Without such a software design, it will be impossible to change just one aspect of payroll without affecting other, unrelated operations. Appropriate form also allows engineers to make a change in an area (such as general ledger) that overlaps several others, and have that change correctly propagate to related operations.

Software design that reflects external function implies that there are no fixed rules for good programming technique. For many years, programmers were taught that global variables and GOTO statements are poor programming practice. In some situations though, these constructs may be exactly what the software needs to marry form with function. It would be incorrect to propose the following rule of building construction: "Always use teak wood instead of pine." Teak is an excellent wood, but sometimes pine is the right choice. In the same way, the right question about a programming technique is, "Is this an appropriate design for the external features we are trying to achieve?"

System Minimality

Imagine a house being built on a street that contains public water supply and electrical service. Now suppose the builders of the house dig a private well and construct their own power generating station. On asking them why they did this, they reply, "We wanted our own well, so it would be just the way we like it. And we didn't know there was already electricity on the street." This extra work and expense in building a house would be terrible! There is nothing wrong with including a well or power generation at a house – if the home really needs them. It is horrible design to include them for little reason or out of ignorance about the public services. Good building design keeps the building as small as possible, by using available external resources.

Beautiful software follows the same principle – it is as small as it can be, by using existing computing resources where possible. It is the responsibility of every software architect and engineer to understand the computing system they are using, and to take advantage of its facilities whenever possible. Software should contain just what it needs to, but no more.

Early in my career, I worked on a project that exemplified everything that can be wrong with software in this regard. The project was a financial information system on Digital VAX minicomputers. In dozens of places throughout the code we chose to "roll our own" method of doing something, rather than use a facility built into the VAX. We wrote our own sorting procedures, screen input/output package, source code control, and automated build tools – all of which were provided on the VAX. I am embarrassed to admit we even wrote our own run-time debugger – although the VAX contained an excellent one. In each case our reason was hubris, ignorance, or laziness to learn more about the computer we were using. The resulting system was many times larger than it needed to be, ran slowly, took a long time to create, and cost far too much money.

Component Singularity

In general, beautiful buildings contain one room for each purpose, and that room gets the function correct.

For example, in most houses there is one master bedroom, which contains everything the room needs. It would be exceedingly poor design for a house to contain four master bedrooms because the builders could not make any of them complete. Or worse, if the builders forgot they had already created a master bedroom and built another one, then forgot about the second and built another, etc.

Of course, some large buildings may *require* more than one space of each type. For example, an office building with 5000 workers may need more than one cafeteria. It is poor architecture, however, to unnecessarily duplicate a space.

In the same way, well-designed software generally contains one instance of each component, and makes the component work correctly. The opposite of this is redundancy and is well recognized as poor software architecture. To cite a specific example, imagine a software system that contains three drivers for one printer. Any change to the printer would require changes to three pieces of software. It is remarkable, however, how many software systems contain unnecessary redundant code. In many cases, this is because one programmer does not know that another engineer already solved the same problem. (Just as the house builders forgot they already had a master bedroom.)

Functional Locality

Good building design places related items together. The equipment and supplies for preparing meals usually are in one room. Plumbing, electrical and heating devices often are together in the basement. The coat closet is near the front door. Of course, houses do not have to be designed this way. A house could be built with a refrigerator in the attic, an oven in the living room, and a dishwasher in the bedroom – but it would be poor design to do so.

Good software follows the same principle of placing related items together. When software is constructed this way, it is easy for members of the project team to understand the software – because the structure makes sense. It is easy to fix bugs and make changes – because the relevant code is located in an obvious place. It is easier to replace an entire feature with a new approach – because there is one distinct piece to replace.

Functional locality implies levels of abstraction. Each room in a house has a purpose, with related items for that purpose in the room. At a broader view though, good building architecture places related rooms together. Rooms for daytime use often are at one end of a house or on one floor. Rooms for nighttime use are at the other end of the house or upstairs. Office buildings place mechanical infrastructure rooms in one area, away from business people.

Good software architecture also uses levels of abstraction to achieve functional locality. In an operating system, all the low-level code for audio effects (sound) should be in one place. Within each higher-level feature (such as the file system), the code for *those* sound effects should be together. Moving up a level, the code for related features (such as file display and Internet Explorer in Windows) should be together.

Readability

It is possible to have two different versions of a software program that function in exactly the same way, and have the same internal design and construction from a technical perspective, but which are vastly different in their human readability. Consider these examples, loosely based on Visual Basic.

Code Fragment A

```
Const MIN_AGE = 0
Const MAX_AGE = 120
Const RETIREMENT_AGE = 65

Dim AgeString As String
Dim AgeNumber As Integer
Dim YearsToRetirement As Integer

EnterAge:
AgeString = Inputbox$("Enter your age.", "Age?", "")
AgeNumber = Cint(AgeString)

If AgeNumber < MIN_AGE Or AgeNumber > MAX_AGE Then
    Msgbox "Age should be between " & _
    MIN_AGE & " and " & MAX_AGE & "."
    Goto EnterAge
End If

If AgeNumber < RETIREMENT_AGE Then
    YearsToRetirement = RETIREMENT_AGE - AgeNumber
Else
    YearsToRetirement = 0
End If
```

Code Fragment B

```
Const xyz=0
Dim x As String,A2 As Integer,Y As Integer
        Const m =120
Const A=65
L47: x=Inputbox$("Enter your age.", "Age?", "")
```

```
A2=Cint(x)
    If A2<xyz Or A2>m Then
Msgbox "Age should be between " & _
xyz & " and " & m & "."
Goto L47
End If
If A2 < A Then
    Y= A-A2
        Else
Y=0
    End If
```

A close inspection reveals that these code fragments are identical, in a strict sense. Based on the other metrics in this article, they have the same overall quality. But if our goal is for real people to maintain and extend real software systems, then we must judge the first fragment to be superior to the second. If a software system is not readable, then it is hard (or impossible) to debug it, modify it, extend it, scale it, etc.

There are two aspects to software readability: clarity that is built into the code, and comments that annotate the code. The first includes meaningful names for variables and constants, good use of white space and indenting, transparent control structures, and straight-line normal execution paths. Good commenting practice stresses comments that educate the next programmer about topics that cannot be gleaned from the code itself, such as the *intention* of each module. (Steve McConnell has written an excellent discussion of this topic in Chapter 19 of his book *Code Complete.*)

Readability of software source code maps directly to the building concepts of design clarity and documentation. The blueprints for a building are not the building itself, and are not strictly needed to keep the building upright once the structure is completed. But blueprints are immensely helpful for maintaining the building over the following years. Any addition or alteration to a building makes crucial use of blueprints and other design documentation. Can a second floor be added to a house using the existing support members? This question is relatively easy to answer with a good set of blueprints, and potentially difficult without the drawings. Can a certain software feature be extended to cover a new situation? Again, this question is much easier to answer if the source code is readable.

Pushing the analogy further, plumbing and electrical systems that are well laid-out and clearly labeled aid anyone attempting to maintain or extend them. An electrical panel may operate fine if it is a mess, but it sure is easier to work on if it is neat.

If other software developers cannot make sense of an engineer's source code, then the code effectively does not contain any of the other metrics discussed here. The qualities may be present in some technical sense, but their impenetrability makes them nonexistent for practical purposes. For example, suppose that a set of source files exhibits perfect minimality (non-redundancy). But if no human can find the single section of source code that relates to a certain feature, no one will be able to fix bugs there or extend the feature in any way.

Simplicity

Software should do its work and solve its problems in the simplest manner possible. In many ways, simplicity is the most important principle of all and overlaps all the other principles.

Simple software is beautiful. Beautiful software is simple. Simple programs have fewer bugs (because there are fewer lines of code which can be wrong), run faster (because there are fewer machine instructions), are smaller (because there is less compiled code), and are easier to fix when broken (because there are fewer places where a bug can occur). Simple programs are dramatically less expensive to create and maintain, for all of the above reasons.

The simplicity of software also is a key metric for distinguishing programming ability.

- Junior programmers can create simple solutions to simple problems.

- Senior programmers can create complex solutions to complex problems.

- Great programmers create simple solutions to complex problems.

The code written by topnotch programmers may appear obvious, once it is finished, but it is vastly more difficult to create.

Just as the goal of science is to find simplicity and order in a seemingly complex universe, the goal of programming should be to find simple solutions to complex problems.

Putting It Together

Finally, there is a global quality to beautiful software that is not the sum of the previous attributes. All of the above qualities must come together to create an overall design that is beautiful. Such beauty cannot be obtained by following a rigid set of guidelines based on the above principles – even though each is important. Just as house architects cannot design beautiful buildings simply by including known elements that have worked elsewhere, good software design is more than a collection of programming techniques that make sense on their own.

Beautiful software is achieved by creating a "wonderful whole" which is more than the sum of its parts. Beautiful software is the right solution, both internally and externally, to the problem at hand.

The result of good software design is a program that is better by many measures; it is not just better in the abstract. Compared to a poor solution, well-designed software meets users' needs more closely, can be completed more quickly, works more reliably, and costs less initially and throughout its life.

All of us in the software world have accepted poor software architecture too often. We should demand the same level of quality in software systems as we do in the buildings where we live and work.

Afterword

Following the initial publication of this article on Slashdot, I received many interesting replies. As is common on that site, the comments ran the gamut from complimentary to scathing. In the hundreds I read, two general threads emerged. One missed a major point of the article, but the other showed an insight I had overlooked.

The first recurring comment was that software development is simply more difficult than other kinds of engineering and, therefore, cannot be judged by the same standards. In this view, creating software is harder than creating any kind of physical structure, so we cannot expect software to have the same high quality as many bridges and office buildings. (Closely related is the assertion that we cannot expect software to be completed on time and on budget, as physical construction often is.) In my opinion, such a viewpoint highlights the worst qualities of software developers.

We think we operate on a higher plane of activity than our mechanical and structural engineering brethren. We think the sorry state of software engineering – cancelled projects, low quality, and missed budgets – is because we do something that is harder than other engineers. The fault, we believe, is not with us, so there is little we can do to improve the performance of software development teams. This is a convenient point of view, if it were true. Unfortunately, it is baloney.

A close look at complex projects tackled by other engineering disciplines shows that these undertakings are every bit as difficult as software development problems. An excellent example is found in a PBS documentary about the 1990 building of the Clark Bridge over the Mississippi River. Watching the constraints and challenges faced by the designers and construction crew is just like viewing a documentary about a large software development project. The bridge had it all – new engineering techniques, time and budget constraints, and unexpected disasters – just like the hurdles faced by a team of programmers trying to beat a competitor to market. Any software developer who thinks our field has special problems should watch this film.

The second recurring comment concerned my discussion about the readability of software source code. In the article I originally stated, "Readability is the one area of software aesthetics that does not have an obvious parallel with physical construction." I went on to explain that source code readability nonetheless is important and stated why this is so. That section of the article bothered me when I wrote it, because it did not fit with my overall analogy between software development and physical construction. Many readers kindly jumped in to defend my analogy and point out my error to not include readability under its umbrella.

The most commonly cited example about construction "readability" was blueprints. Readers pointed out that a well-built building still requires blueprints to reveal its internal structure, just as well-designed software still needs clarifying comments. If we want to modify a building, the blueprints help us find the right places to cut and nail, just as source code comments help us with debugging.

Another example from readers of construction readability was color-coded wires and circuit breaker labels. A perfectly made electrical system in a house is still confusing (and dangerous) without consistent use of the black/white wiring convention. An electrical panel is impossible to understand without labels stating which circuit breaker is for the second-floor bathroom and which is for the garage.

These ideas about readability apply to software also. A great design is made even better by comments that help the next programmer to understand it.

Resources

- pbs.org/wgbh/nova/bridge (Clark Bridge)
- stevemcconnell.com/books (*Code Complete*)
- catb.org/esr/writings/taoup/html/ch01s06.html (Eric Raymond's essay *Basics of Unix Philosophy*, which contains similar ideas)

The Missing Theory of Refactoring

Refactoring is an incremental change to software source code which improves the design of the program, without altering the behavior of the program.

By "design" we mean a human-readable abstraction of the software: source code, diagrams of source code, calling sequences, data flow, and broad descriptions of large software systems (architecture). By "behavior" we are referring to the semantics that matter to the program's users. Intuitively, we want the software to "do the same thing" from the users' point of view, before and after refactoring. We don't care if the modified source code causes the compiler to generate different machine code.

A simple example of refactoring is Split Temporary Variable. This change is applied to a variable that has been reused for more than one purpose, and splits it into two or more variables, each with a single, clear use. The new variables are easier to understand and debug because each has only one meaning. After this refactoring, the program has a better design and is more readable.

Why is refactoring interesting or valuable? There are at least three reasons.

1. A series of small refactorings can produce significant improvements to existing code. While each individual refactoring is minor, applying a dozen refactorings, each on top of the others, can result in a much improved software design. The improvement can transform confusing, poorly-written software into well-designed and readable code.

2. Refactoring lightens the load on the design phase of software development. The standard advice to spend lots of time on design, before writing any code, is based on the assumption that it is hard to fix a bad design later in the programming process. But refactoring allows us to worry less about the up-front design phase, and begin programming sooner. (This is not an argument to spend no time

on design, or to proceed with a lousy design, but refactoring makes design errors easier to fix later.)

3. Refactoring leads to a more realistic design phase. The goal of producing an excellent design up front, that is correct throughout the life of the software, is certainly well-intentioned. It would be great if humans were capable of doing this. But the reality is we are not. We cannot anticipate design bugs that may arise or the changes users will request once they begin interacting with the software. Refactoring allows us to say, "We will do the best job we can now with design and architecture, but we recognize that these macro views of the software may need to change later."

It is important to note that there is nothing new about the idea of looking at software source code, finding ways to improve it, and then making those changes. Programmers have been doing this for as long as people have created software. Simple "debugging" often involves a structural change to the code, not just a one-line fix, and any positive structural change is essentially refactoring.

As a separate topic of study, however, refactoring got its start in the early 1990s with a PhD thesis by Bill Opdyke, *Refactoring Object-Oriented Frameworks*. In 1999, Martin Fowler wrote *Refactoring: Improving the Design of Existing Code*, which became the de-facto standard book on the subject. Refactoring is now an accepted software engineering discipline, included in many of the field's conferences and journals.

Any discussion of refactoring should mention the crucial role of automated tools. The reason tools are key is that applying even a single, straightforward source code transformation to a large program is a tedious, error-prone task. Imagine applying the common transformation Encapsulate Field across a large code base. You have to find all read-only references to the (previously) public field, replace each with a Get() method call, then find all write-references to the field, and replace those with Set() calls. For a field with a thousand references, this is a pain in the neck, unless there is a tool to help. For more complex changes, such as Move Method (between classes), the task is even more daunting.

No one will refactor anything if programmers hate doing it. There has been considerable work in the tools area, both theoretical and practical. As examples, both the Eclipse Java and NetBeans IDEs include automated support for some common refactoring transformations.

I must confess that when I first learned about refactoring I thought it was a trivial re-statement of techniques experienced programmers understand implicitly. I was shocked that anyone would receive a PhD for describing this knowledge. It is true that much of refactoring is obvious, in a general sense, to good programmers. But I did not understand the significant impact on software design and development that comes from a disciplined approach to refactoring. (And when I took the trouble to actually read Opdyke's dissertation, I realized it is more than a re-statement of a few programming tricks.) Despite the successes of the refactoring movement, and its track record helping programmers on real-world projects, the whole endeavor has some glaring open problems.

1. *How does a programmer know when to refactor?* Software developers spend many hours looking at thousands of lines of code. On good projects, most of the code is decent and well-designed. So what parts should be refactored? The available automated tools generally do not help with this question. Most tools assist by correctly *doing* a transformation, after the programmer has decided to do it. But how can a programmer *find* code to refactor?

2. *Which refactoring should be applied in a given situation?* There are at least 70 standard refactorings for object-oriented software. For a specific section of source code, only some of these 70 make sense of course. But, of the transformations that could be applied in a specific place, which one is best?

3. *Why is refactoring an improvement to software?* It cannot be the case that each individual transformation is an improvement, because many transformations contradict each other. For example, Extract Class and Inline Class perform exact opposite changes. If each always improves software, we can just apply the

two transformations to the same class, in an endless cycle, improving the software forever. Instead, every refactoring transformation improves software *sometimes*, in the right situation. But why?

Taking some liberties to summarize thousands of pages of research, the current answers to these questions are:

1. A section of source code should be refactored when it "smells bad."
2. For each bad smell, we should apply one of the refactorings that tend to help with this malodor.
3. No one knows.

For a better answer to these questions, we need a *theory* of refactoring, to explain what refactoring is, why some code smells bad, and why refactoring makes software better. It just so happens I have such a theory. My theory may not be correct, but science advances by proposing strong, predictive theories and then testing their consequences.

In 2002, I wrote an essay titled *Beautiful Software* that presents an overall theory of software design. I argued that there are seven general principles of good software design. The principles describe properties of the software itself, not ways of creating software. It does not matter if the software is created with Extreme Programming, CMMI Level 5, Java, or COBOL. The principles are asserted as universal properties of all good software. In summary, they are:

Cooperation – Software should work well with its surrounding environment, which is the computer hardware, operating system, middleware (such as database and security layers) and applications.

Appropriate form – The internal design of software should reflect and create its external behavior; form should follow function.

Minimality – Software should be as small as it can be, by using other computing resources wherever possible. Software should contain just what it needs to, but no more.

Singularity – Good software contains one instance of each component, and makes that component work correctly. The opposite of singularity is redundancy, widely recognized as poor design.

Locality – Source code should place related items together. This makes it easy to fix bugs and make changes, because programmers can quickly find the code they want. Functional locality implies levels of abstraction, and locality should be achieved at each level of description.

Readability – There are two aspects to software readability: clarity that is built into the code, and comments that annotate the code. The first includes meaningful names for variables and constants, good use of white space and indenting, and transparent control structures. Good commenting educates the next programmer about the *intention* of each module.

Simplicity – Software should do its work and solve its problems in the simplest manner possible. In many ways, simplicity is the most important principle of all and overlaps all the others. Simple programs have fewer bugs, run faster, are smaller, and are easier to fix when broken. Simple programs are dramatically less expensive to create and maintain for these reasons.

In view of this theory, what is refactoring? Refactoring is an attempt to bring software more in line with these general principles of good design. What is a bad smell? A bad smell is the absence of one of the design tenets. A really bad odor is caused by breaking several design principles at once. A given refactoring transformation applies in certain situations (pre-conditions) to improve the software's compliance with good design.

For example, consider the known bad smells "switch statement" and "duplicated code". Both result from violating the principle of component singularity. These smells are just special cases of the more general problem of missing singularity. In the same way, the smells "feature envy", "data clumps", "shotgun surgery", and "parallel inheritance" are all special cases of missing functional locality. The transformations that are known to remove these smells work because they move the software toward restoration of the broken underlying design principles.

I assert that every refactoring transformation has between one and seven real effects, each effect being the improvement of one of the design criteria from my theory. I assert that there are really only seven basic smells, one for breaking each design principle.

Current refactoring literature presents the transformations and smells ad hoc; they might be valid, but there is no apparent scheme or explanation for them. The seven design principles solve this problem by providing a theoretical foundation for refactoring.

The relationship between refactoring and the design guidelines is like the relationship between the substances of the world and the periodic table. There are seemingly thousands of different kinds of "stuff" on earth. There is dirt and sand and fire and snow and water and plants and trees and animals, etc. But the discovery of elements and the organization of the periodic table changed this belief dramatically by saying, "There are actually only a small number of elements, which combine in myriad ways to form the thousands of things in our world." By Occam's Razor, a simpler theory (elements) is preferred over a theory with additional constructs (everything is different).

In the same way, the seven software design principles combine in many variations to form all the refactoring smells and their correcting transformations.

So here are answers to the questions I posed.

1. *How does a programmer know when to refactor?* Refactor when software violates one or more of the seven principles of good design.

2. *Which refactoring should be applied in a given situation?* Use the transformation that most easily reestablishes good design where it is currently broken.

3. *Why is refactoring an improvement to software?* There are universal principles of good software design, and the proper refactoring helps software conform to these guidelines.

• • •

As any theory should, the software design principles also suggest undiscovered phenomena: new bad smells and new refactorings to correct them. Confirmation of the existence of these phenomena is evidence that the theory is correct. (This approach is common in physics. A theory predicts certain behavior. When the behavior is observed experimentally, it supports the truth of the theory.)

For software, a new bad smell predicted by the design rules is "reinvents the wheel", which violates the principle of minimality. An example of this odor is the common practice by programmers of writing their own sort routines. Since many operating- and middleware-systems provide highly-optimized sorting services, a new sort method can unnecessarily increase the total size of a software product. A new refactoring transformation to remove this smell is Replace With System Service. This refactoring is applied by completely removing a long run of code (or a method or class) and replacing it with the invocation of a built-in feature. Used appropriately, it is clear this change is an improvement to software.

In addition to this example, I suspect the seven software design principles predict other bad smells and transformations to correct them, and that confirmation of these predictions will further support the theory. I leave this as a topic for future articles and other researchers.

Resources

- amazon.com/dp/0201485672/ (Martin Fowler's book on refactoring)
- refactoring.com
- en.wikipedia.org/wiki/Code_refactoring
- science.howstuffworks.com/innovation/occams-razor.htm

All Source Code Should Be Open

Most software is poorly designed and built. This statement comes as no surprise to many in the software industry and is elucidated well by Charles Mann in his popular article *Why Software Is So Bad*. But even if everyone accepts the assertion that software generally stinks, there is still a problem. How do we get software designers and programmers to raise the quality of their work?

Few people ever see the actual software product – source code – so what would motivate engineers to do better? My answer is that source code should be a standard part of every commercial software release. This single change would have a profound impact on the quality of software systems worldwide.

When you drive across a bridge, its design is open for inspection. You can see the overall structure, the method used to anchor the cables, the thickness of the roadbed, and so forth. If you want a closer look, you can walk the bridge and see more detail. The same is true of housing construction and automobile design. You can see both the outward appearance and the inner structure of these engineering products. With a little effort and some background knowledge, it is possible to independently evaluate the design and construction of these objects. Some internal parts may require extra work to see, such as underwater bridge pilings, roof trusses, or automobile crankshafts. In principle, though, there is nothing to stop you from examining them, and experts routinely do so.

Software, on the other hand, is a crucial piece of engineering that is shrouded in secrecy. Experienced software developers cannot look into the source code of Raytheon's air traffic control system, Windows 7, or a dental X-ray machine to see how they are built. We cannot see the number and depth of comments in the code, the calling sequence of the routines, the clarity of the variable names, or the simplicity of the executable statements. This fact makes software vastly different from other important products. We cannot see whether we are buying junk or quality.

The physical equivalent of hidden source code would be a new bridge with all structural parts encased in impenetrable black plastic, and the builders asking us to trust them that everything is okay. As a public safety measure, we never would allow this. Similarly, few people would buy a house if the contractor refused to allow a home inspection prior to the sale. Unfortunately, this is how we buy software. Software systems have a huge global importance, but their structures are hidden from independent inspection.

This secrecy is the key reason we have unacceptable software. Software designers, programmers, and managers get away with bad code because no one outside their small workgroup ever sees it. Developers write code they are ashamed of because they are pretty sure no one will look at it. Managers encourage engineers to write "quick and dirty" code to meet the next project milestone, with confidence they will not be held accountable for their part in the poor result. I have personally witnessed these actions and suspect most other software professionals have as well. Commercial software is filled with bad design, horrible coding style, inefficient algorithms, and snide comments (or no comments at all).

The solution is to release all software with a copy of its source code. This is currently the practice with nearly every other engineering discipline, because their designs are open for visual inspection and physical testing.

In addition, each software developer, designer, and manager should attach their name to the sections of code they work on. All code (good or bad) would be traceable to the people who created it. This sunshine policy would improve software quality for two reasons. Everyone involved in the software creation process would take more pride in their work because their names would be on the code. And any buyer who cared to could inspect the source code to make sure they were getting good quality. Of course, not every software buyer has the expertise to perform this inspection, but some do.

I can picture software executives everywhere clutching their chests in horror at this proposal. What about intellectual property rights? Wouldn't software companies engage in widespread theft of each other's hard work? No, they wouldn't, for several reasons. First, re-using intellectual property is not as easy as it seems. Second, software is covered by copyright and patents laws. Third, the source code release could be modified in clever ways to make its re-use difficult.

Consider the novels of Tom Clancy. The implementation of his writing (the words on the page) and the underlying structure (thematic development, characterization, and so on) are fully open for anyone to inspect. There is nothing obvious to prevent me from stealing these items for my own novel. In practice, however, there are many barriers to my doing so. It is not easy to produce good writing just because I have read some. If this were so simple, I would write like Shakespeare or Steinbeck, which I do not. Also, someone else's writing may not plug cleanly into what I am trying to accomplish in my novel. Mr. Clancy has plenty of ways to punish me should I write a book that has the same story line or characters as one of his bestsellers. The fact that this system works is illustrated by the problems of historian Doris Kearns Goodwin, whose career was nearly wrecked by accusations of plagiarism.

Stealing software is just as difficult as stealing literature, for the same reasons. Reading Knuth does not make me as good a programmer as he. It is notoriously difficult to plug software fragments from one program into another, as is shown by the frustrations of the software reuse movement.

Software companies have the same copyright protection for their source code as novelists do for their writing. And software has the protection of the patent system, which is not available to writers, poets and musicians. Neither of these bodies of law is perfect of course, but the threat of their use is a strong deterrent to theft of source code.

The third way that companies can guard against improper re-use of their source code is by strategically omitting a few key pieces. Leaving out the constant definitions (#define, const, public static final) from a source code tree makes it impossible to re-compile or to steal easily. The source code is still eminently readable, but hard to re-purpose. Going further, a source tree could omit a small number of very key routines, perhaps the "crown jewels" of the most important algorithms. Again, the overall source code would be highly readable, but the central intellectual property is kept secret.

This final method, of small key omissions, will help with the problem of international software piracy, where U.S. laws are ineffective.

Note that I am not advocating open source licensing for commercial software. This is an important point. Companies and other organizations can still own their source code, just as Tom Clancy is the owner of his writing even though his words have appeared in public. The licenses for source code can be as restrictive or permissive as each company chooses. But the source code would be visible to buyers.

Software businesses now are fiercely protective of their source code, treating it as the holy of holies. Companies claim they do this to guard their property. In fact, the real reason often is that the software is so bad it is embarrassing.

If IBM, Raytheon, Microsoft, Oracle, etc. are producing good software products – as they claim – let's see the code.

Resources

- technologyreview.com/computing/12887/ (*Why Software Is So Bad*, by Charles Mann)
- www.slate.com/id/2091197/ (Doris Kearns Goodwin plagiarism)
- copyright.gov/circs/circ61.pdf (copyright of software)
- ipwatchdog.com/ (patents for software)

Is Software Patentable?

I am a software engineer who writes about that topic and other related areas of computer science. Recently, I published an article titled *Software Engineering Is More Than Computer Science* which discusses the differences between programming and formal (mathematical) computer science[1]. In response to that article, IPWatchdog.com kindly invited me to comment about some of the controversy surrounding patents for software.

My position is that software *must* be patentable, or 500 years of patent laws make no sense.

---

1   It is not necessary to read that chapter before this one.

First, some well-established background principles:

- Novel, useful manufacturing processes can be patented. Among many examples are US Patent No. 7,000,318, which relates to a method of designing and manufacturing vehicles; and US Patent No. 5,194,877, which relates to a process for manufacturing thermal ink jet printheads.

- Novel, useful electronic devices can be patented. Examples include US Patent No. 5,867,795, which relates to a portable electronic device having a transceiver and visual display; and US Patent No. 5,557,579, which relates to a power-up circuit.

- Just because something is a clever, interesting, original piece of software does not automatically make it patentable. The primary example is software that is a mere expression of a mathematical formula, because mathematical truths are not patentable.

The reason that software must be patentable is that software can be an inseparable part of both manufacturing processes and electronic devices. A patent for such items must crucially include the software components of the invention, or the patent would be incomplete.

Consider two imaginary manufacturing processes, MP1 and MP2. Both produce a new type of automobile which is vastly more reliable than existing cars. These new cars only need minor maintenance every 10 years, and run well for at least 100 years. MP1 achieves this astonishing result partly by using better raw materials, but primarily through improved manufacturing processes. The inventors figured out how to organize workers on an assembly line in a much better way, to create much better cars. MP1 would, of course, be patentable.

MP2 creates the same cars as MP1, using the same materials. But MP2 replaces the people on the assembly line with robots. The robots are controlled by a large, complex software system. The software instructs the robots to inspect the materials, reject parts that are defective, and then assemble a car as good as MP1 creates. If MP1 is patentable, then MP2 must be also, especially if MP2 were invented first.

What would a patent for MP2 cover? It would contain a description of the raw materials, an explanation of how the plant floor is laid out, a list of the robots used, and, crucially, the software instructions to operate the robots correctly. If the owners of MP2 were to sell or license this process, what would they deliver to the buyer? Among other things, the deliverable would contain a printout or computer disk with the robotic software. Without this software, MP2 cannot make a single car and has no monetary value.

Now consider two electronic devices, ED1 and ED2. Assume both are single-chip integrated circuits that

perform identical operations, but their internal constructions are different. ED1 is "hardwired". It contains
thousands of transistors, resistors, and other embedded
circuits, arranged to perform the overall operations
of the chip. ED2, on the other hand, contains a pro-
grammable micro-machine and microcode that implement the same operations as ED1. So ED2 achieves the
desired (identical) behavior by software emulation of
the hardwired components of ED1.

For those unfamiliar with digital electronics, ED2 might
seem hard to believe. In fact, hardware emulation by
microcode, in exactly the way I describe, is common
today. So if ED1 is potentially patentable, ED2 must
be as well, especially if ED2 were invented before ED1.
And what would a patent for ED2 cover? The patent
would include the operations of ED2, perhaps its physical characteristics, and, of course, its microcode. By any
definition, microcode is software.

Finally, consider a third device, ED3. This device is physically identical to ED2, both externally and internally. It
is housed in the same integrated circuit chip. It contains
the same layers of silicon and germanium, creating the
same set of transistors, resistors and other internal components. In other words, ED3 contains the same micro-
machine as ED2.

But ED3 performs a very different function than ED2.
It takes different inputs and gives different outputs. It
performs operations for which no previous integrated

circuit was available. It solves a long-standing problem in a novel, non-obvious way. ED3 does this because it contains a new micro-program for its embedded micro-machine. ED3 is the same as ED2, except for its software. And that software makes ED3 a new device, which meets the criteria for patentability.

As mentioned above, new, useful software is not always patentable. But *some* software must be patentable, or the long history of patents for manufacturing process and electronic devices cannot be sustained as software becomes central to these inventions.

Resources

- google.com/patents/about?id=pA53AAAAEBAJ (patent for manufacturing vehicles)
- google.com/patents/about?id=COwlAAAAEBAJ (patent for manufacturing inkjet heads)
- google.com/patents/about?id=N7gXAAAAEBAJ (patent for portable electronic device)
- google.com/patents/about?id=L38fAAAAEBAJ (patent for power-up circuit)
- uspto.gov/web/offices/pac/mpep/documents/2100_2106_02.htm (mathematical truths not patentable)
- en.wikipedia.org/wiki/Microcode

MANAGEMENT OF SOFTWARE PROJECTS

A Software Schedule Ain't Nothin' but a Piece of Paper

The original deadline for our software project had come and gone, and every week the new finish date was sliding farther into the future. The Vice President of Development decided that he needed to call a project summit meeting, bring the finish date in sooner, and nail down a schedule once and for all. He called all the important managers (but none of the programmers) into a room. They shut the door and vowed not to emerge until they had shortened the schedule.

One of the managers laid a rock on the table, solemnly turned it over, and said they should "leave no stone unturned" in their effort to shave time off the schedule. They re-examined each task in the project list, shortened many of them, made some tasks concurrent, and eliminated a few others. They emerged several hours later with a tightened schedule, and an earlier end date.

All the managers were happy. They had accomplished their goal of shortening the schedule.

In hindsight, it is not surprising what happened – the managers' effort was a waste of time. The new schedule had no effect at all on the pace of development. The project was finished at about the same time it would have been, except that five or six highly-paid people wasted a half-day looking at a rock in a room.

Another true story... I worked on a project to create a new banking ATM machine to compete with the established vendor. This was a complex hardware/software undertaking, using an embedded processor board, a cash dispenser mechanism, a deposit-taking device, a receipt printer, a screen, and a communication link to the bank's mainframe. The software was written in assembly language, and we debugged the code with an in-circuit CPU emulator (itself a complicated device). Not surprisingly, this project schedule started slipping also. Upper management, in another city, was not happy.

So, our local manager began keeping two versions of the project schedule. He kept an "official" version, with an aggressive completion date, which he reported out to his boss at headquarters; and a "real" version that he kept in his desk drawer. He assured us that he only expected us to work toward the schedule in his drawer.

These stories are humorous, in a Pointy-Haired-Boss way, but they raise an important question that haunts many software projects: What is the relationship between software schedules and reality? In the second example above, there was clearly no relationship, and the official schedule was useful only for doodling and wrapping fish. But how about honest schedules that all team members really hope reflect an actual completion date?

In my experience on software teams, both large and small, and in my academic research, I have found that there are some common factors that lead to a reliable schedule. Ignoring these factors may turn your project into fodder for eye-rolling party conversation years later.

Completion dates can only be refined as a project moves along.

The classic view of software development is to perform all of the design and planning at the start, estimate a completion date, and then begin programming. This would be a great method for software development... if it worked. A more realistic approach is cyclical development, which repeats the design, time estimation, programming, testing, and delivery phases, many times over. Steve McConnell and Barry Boehm advocate such iterative development and refer to schedule refinement as "narrowing the cone of uncertainty." Agile development takes this idea further and estimates work in very short chunks, finishing and delivering each phase, before estimating the next small set of development tasks.

Everyone in the software world would love to pin down completion dates and total costs at the start of each development project, but it is probably beyond human ability to do so.

Reliable schedules are based on commitment (buy-in) from all participants.

Participants include management, marketing, architects, programmers, testers, and the documentation team, among others. The meeting I described at the beginning of this article did not include anyone actually doing the hands-on project tasks, dooming the meeting (and its resulting schedule) to failure. Buy-in means active participation in planning, project design, and estimating. It does not mean getting people to agree to a schedule because they fear for their jobs if they do not.

There is a subtle danger about buy-in, however, that you must guard against. Most people want to perform well–especially young, motivated engineers eager to show their programming chops. Software team members may voluntarily commit to a schedule, which they truly believe in, even when that schedule is unrealistic. The key ingredient to accurate estimates is *informed* consent, based on sufficient experience with projects of this type.

Accurate schedules are based on the experience of the same team, using the same technologies, solving similar problems.

This is the most frustrating part of software estimation, and requires a large ego check by technical people when looking at a new project. Programmers tend to think that the new project is not much different from something they have done before. The thinking goes, "I have been working with Java for two years, so this new Java project shouldn't be hard" or "We have put up an e-commerce site on an Apache HTTP Server before, so it will be easy to do it again."

The reality is that even if everyone on your team has a computer science degree and ten years of programming experience, new software projects are often *very* different than previous projects.

Consider the following scenario from outside of the software world.... A commercial building company is experienced and fast at constructing standard office buildings between three and ten floors tall, using a steel frame, brick exterior, open interior design, on stable bedrock sites. They can confidently and accurately predict the time and cost for constructing another such building, with minor variations from their previous projects. Now imagine that you ask this company to construct a hospital that is 100 stories tall, using a radical tilting design, on top of a seismic fault. The hospital is to be built from standard steel and bricks.

The construction company would make a major blunder if they thought they could provide a time and price estimate for this hospital. Even though it uses the same raw materials they normally work with, the design and constructions problems are far outside their scope of expertise (and probably beyond anyone's expertise).

Many software projects suffer from the same *we've done something like this before* problem. A new piece of software written in Java on Linux may not be like anything ever created by humans, even when the team has lots of experience with Java on Linux.

If your software team has built ten compilers, for modern procedural programming languages, generating machine instructions for industry-standard CPUs, and you are asked to build an eleventh such compiler, you can confidently estimate this project. But don't fool yourself into thinking your team is always in this enviable situation; it usually is not. Solving new software problems is *hard,* and they are hard to estimate, even if you have previously used some of the same raw materials.

This is a major point of the CMMI process framework from the Software Engineering Institute at Carnegie Mellon. In their terminology, software schedules are accurate only when the software process is "repeatable."

Conclusion

I know what you might be thinking: "This is nice software engineering theory, Chuck. And it is swell of you to dispense this wisdom from on high. But I have a real project right now, and my boss wants to know how long it is going to take."

Yes, there are real pressures from customers, competitors, and managers. I've been there. Unfortunately, large software projects tend to have a life of their own. The lines of code you are writing don't know that XYZ Corp is about to release a competing product before yours, or that your boss's boss is yelling at you. Wishing that your program will work quickly won't make it so.

Showing up for work each day to battle an impossible project deadline consumes a huge amount of time and energy. Ironically, an ongoing schedule battle takes time *away* from doing a good job on the software. Recognizing that a software project is hard, and hard to estimate accurately, frees you to work on it in a realistic manner.

Resources

- AgileManifesto.org
- www.sei.cmu.edu/cmmi/

It's Not About Lines of Code

Everyone wants programmers to be productive. Managers want maximum productivity – it gets the work done faster and makes the manager look good. Programmers like being productive. They can get home earlier, have reduced stress during the workday, and feel better about their finished products. Programming productivity is even in each country's national interest, since it advances the country's position in the world-wide software industry.

Unfortunately, the standard definitions of software productivity are incorrect. They miss the essence of software

development. This article examines some of the usual
definitions for programmer productivity, shows why
they are wrong, and then proposes an alternate definition that accurately captures what programming is
really about.

Lines of code per day – This is the classic definition of
software productivity for individual programmers.
Unfortunately, as other authors have noted as well, the
definition makes little sense. Imagine a programmer
named Fred Fastfinger who writes 5000 lines of code,
on average, each workday. Now assume Fred's code is
of such poor quality that, for each day of work he completes, someone else must spend five days debugging
the code. Is Fred highly productive? Certainly not. What
we want is many lines of *good* code.

Lines of correct code per day – This definition adjusts for
the problem of a programmer producing lousy code. In
the above example, using the new definition, Fred's productivity becomes 833 lines/day (5000 lines, divided by
one person-day to write the code plus five person-days
to fix it). But even this definition is lacking. Suppose
Fred cleans up his act and begins to produce 1000 lines
of correct code per day by himself. Imagine his code is
completely bug-free, but contains no comments at all.
Is Fred productive now? Probably not. The code may
be correct based on the current specification, but we
know software requirements always change. The next
programmer to take over Fred's code will find it impenetrable, and possibly will be forced to rewrite the code

in order to add any new features. (Even Fred will likely find his code opaque in a few months.)

Lines of correct, well-documented code per day – This definition gets closer to what we want, but something still is missing. Imagine both Fred and another programmer, Danny Designer, are given similar assignments. Fred now writes comments and he completes his program by writing 1000 lines of well-documented, correct code per day for five days, for a total of 5000 lines. Danny also completes his assignment in five days, but he writes only 500 lines of code per day (all correct and well-documented) for a total of 2500 lines. Who was more productive? Probably Danny. His code is shorter and simpler, and simplicity is almost always better in engineering. Danny's code probably will be easier to extend and modify, and likely will have a longer lifespan, because of its compactness.

Lines of clean, simple, correct, well-documented code per day – This is a pretty good definition of productivity, and one many experienced, savvy technical managers would accept. But there is still something about this definition that misses what software engineers ultimately are trying to do.

Imagine that Fred, Danny, and a third programmer, Ingrid Insightful, are given similar assignments. Fred and Danny head right to their desks and begin writing good code. Something about the assignment bothers Ingrid however, so she decides to go outside for a walk.

After a lap around the park, she buys a decaf mochaccino, sips a little, and lies down under a tree.

Soon Ingrid falls asleep and starts dreaming about a
giant, green blob of software that is attacking her. She
fights back with a sword. During the fight, she hacks
off parts of the blob, which then lie quivering on the
ground. The main blob attacks again, and Ingrid wakes
up with a start. Suddenly she knows what is bothering
her about the programming assignment: the new feature is suspiciously similar to an existing feature.

She strolls back indoors, goes to her desk, nods hello
to Fred and Danny, and looks over the code base. Sure
enough, the new feature she was asked to create is actually a generalization of a current special-case feature.

Ingrid opens the source code for the existing feature
and begins deleting large sections of it. Before long, she
has generalized the feature so it is simpler, more intui-
tive, and includes the new capabilities she was asked to
add. In the process, she has reduced the code base by
2000 lines. Around 3:00, Ingrid says goodbye to Fred
and Danny, and heads to her health club to work off the
mochaccino.

Who was more productive on this day? Certainly Ingrid.
Fred and Danny are not even finished yet. Ingrid's new
code works completely, she has simplified the entire
program, and the user interface is improved by reduc-
ing the apparent feature count.

But note that Ingrid's productivity included writing negative 2000 lines of code and spending little time in the office.

While this example may seem fanciful, it is actually quite realistic. Getting away from a problem sometimes is a good way to solve it. And programmers who understand the big picture make smarter decisions, because they are able to reuse code and combine features effectively.

Solving customer problems quickly in an elegant way – This is the true definition of programmer productivity, and is what Ingrid accomplished in the example. I use the term *customer* very loosely. The customer may be a group of users in the same organization, a fighter pilot whose aircraft depends on the software, the world at large (for open source programmers), or yourself when writing a software tool. What software engineering really is about is solving problems for the people who will use the software. Any other definition of programmer productivity misses the mark.

This definition raises a difficult question though: If a programmer can be highly productive by writing a negative amount of code, how do we measure productivity for software engineers? There is no easy answer to this question, but the answer surely is not a rigid formula related to lines of code, bug counts, or face time in the office. Each of these measures has some value for some purposes, but managers should not lose sight of what software engineers are doing. They are creating machines to solve human problems.

Why Software Really Fails, And What to Do About It

What is software? What is it about software that takes so long to create? And why does software development so often go wrong, compared to other kinds of engineering?

Along with my day job as a software consultant, I like to think about the essence of this stuff I work with every day. I wonder why it is different from other "stuff" that humans build things with, such as bricks and steel and chemicals.

Computer scientists have proposed many ways of looking at software, including as a function with inputs and

an output, and as instructions for transforming computer memory from one state to another. I like to think
of software, however, as a machine. It is a machine we
cannot touch, but it is a machine nonetheless. (I am
not the first to suggest this view.) Equivalently, we can
think of software as one part of a machine that includes
the computer hardware, allowing us to see software as a
component of a physical machine.

When we create a new software system we are creating a new machine. The principles that apply to good
machine design also apply to good software design, such
as durability, maintainability, and simplicity. But, if this
is true, why does software development seem harder
than mechanical or structural engineering? After all,
people build airplanes, bridges, skyscrapers and facto-
ries, on time and on budget. (Not always of course, but
often.) It is rare that large physical engineering projects
are simply abandoned half-built, after years of effort,
with millions of dollars spent, left to rust under the elements. But there are many examples of this scale of failure for software projects, including the Denver Airport
baggage handling system, FBI Virtual Case File, and
the IRS modernization effort. Many, many others were
never made public because their failures were hidden
by organizations not wishing to be embarrassed by the
scope of their incompetence.

So what, specifically, is it about software that causes
large software projects to go wrong more often than
with other kinds of engineering? This question has

been examined before, including in the book *Dreaming in Code* and the SEI research project *Patterns of Failure.* Some of the proposed answers are: poor requirements documentation, inadequate training of programmers, and that software is just plain harder than other kinds of engineering. I believe there is another answer, however, which has not been stated clearly.

The problem is not the nature of software; software is just a type of machine and is amenable to known methods for good machine design and project management. The problem is the way we approach software projects and our expectations for their outcomes. In short, we expect too much. Too often we try to "invent the world" with a new software project, instead of relying on well-known designs and methods that are likely to succeed.

Consider this fictional mechanical engineering project that is run like many software projects.

The motivation for this project is that cars are a very poor form of transportation for individual people. This has been widely recognized for a long time. We want a smaller, lighter, cleaner, less expensive device for personal, local transportation.

We will call the new invention "Personal Transportation Device 1000", stating its intended selling price in US Dollars. For individual commuting and errands within 50 miles, we want PTD-1000 to make the current automobile obsolete. We do not want the device to use existing, already congested roads, so PTD-1000 will fly.

Our goals include low fuel cost and no pollution, so the motor will be powered by helium fusion. Fusion is an emerging standard, but we believe that this project will provide synergy with fusion research, both driving the research and serving as a test bed for it.

We want the device to be light, which will contribute to efficiency and allow the single user to pick it up, so we will construct PTD-1000 primarily from Rearden Metal. The design team recognizes that the formulation for this metal is not yet finished, so we will assign our A-team of engineers to finish this work in parallel with the other subsystems.

The final key design criterion is that a person who is physically disabled must be able to enter a building after getting there. So PTD-1000 will convert to a wheelchair for use indoors.

The participants in this project all understand that it is a substantial undertaking, but enthusiasm is high for the benefits that will be realized at its completion. There is buy-in by all stakeholders. The investors and engineers have committed to a budget and to a completion date 18 months from now. Everyone has agreed to forgo their vacations for the next year in order to meet this schedule.

Of course, this fictional invention is absurd. Anyone with common sense can see that it will fail dramatically. But take the above scenario, and substitute software concepts for the physical details, and you have an accurate description of many real software projects.

In contrast to software projects, traditional engineering relies on tried-and-true materials and methods, applied in well-understood ways to new applications. An aeronautical engineer may design a new aircraft that does not look or function exactly like any previous plane, but the structural members, outer skin, wiring components, and engines usually are copies of proven parts and techniques. Manufacturing plants, skyscrapers, roads, and bridges are built with a similar philosophy – substantial reuse of known pieces, put together largely in known ways.

Traditional engineers, of course, sometimes advance the state of their art, by using new materials or techniques or both. The Burj Khalifa building in Dubai recently set a new height record. The engineers did this partly by employing a special formulation of concrete to achieve the weight-bearing strength required, and by pouring the concrete at night to aid in proper hardening. But these innovations are in tightly constrained situations, making incremental improvements to well-studied topics. Concrete has been around for thousands of years in some format and 200+ years in its modern version. New bridges similarly use known methods, with possibly some incremental innovations to solve special problems for that location. The public would not have it any other way.

Software projects often take the opposite approach, attempting to use many radical new materials (data structures) operated on by grossly unproven methods (programming code) to produce a machine that performs a never-before-seen function. Our large software projects often resemble precisely the sort of absurd dream invention described above. Why do we do this?

The reason is that since we cannot see or touch software, it appears that all the parts of software, tested or novel, are quite similar and can be used equally well as machine subassemblies. In fact, software components do not all have the same approximate reliability, not by a long shot. We fail to appreciate fully that well-tested software modules can have a high probability of successful reuse, while novel software components are often a crap-shoot.

When we visualize software as a machine, it becomes clear just how unwise it is to invent too much in a new software system. Picture the overall software as a factory assembly line of robots, or a new kind of automobile. The major software modules are sections of the factory, or important pieces of the automobile. The software subroutines are parts making up the larger mechanical components. Individual lines of source code are single pieces of metal in a robot, or springs, or gears, or levers. Function parameters are rods or lasers reaching into another mechanical subassembly.

When the assembly line or car is started for the first time, the parts may not work together correctly. They may rub or bang into each other, preventing the whole machine from working right. This might occur in hundreds of places. Some problems may not be seen until a certain sequence of actions is attempted simultaneously.

In the same way, a large software project is an incredibly complex machine, with millions of possible interactions among overlapping parts, compounded by interactions of the interactions. The full behavior of many software systems is well beyond human understanding. This is why we cannot accurately predict bugs in complex software; we are trying to build machines we cannot comprehend.

Oversimplifying a bit, there are two common approaches to software projects.

1. Design and build software in a conservative manner, using tried-and-true components, assembled by a stable team of engineers, who have successfully built similar systems. These projects usually can be estimated accurately, and completed on time and budget.

2. Attempt to create software that is substantially new. These are really research projects, not engineering endeavors. They have uncertain outcomes and no reliable time/cost estimates.

An example of #1 is the creation of a new compiler by a software development company that has produced many compilers for dozens of languages and target machines. When this company takes on a new compiler project, for a variation of an existing source language, with a carefully specified target instruction set, by an experienced team of compiler engineers, then this project has a high likelihood of success. Techniques such as reusable class libraries and design patterns help software projects conform to this model.

An example of #2 was FBI's Virtual Case File, previously mentioned. No one had ever created a software system to perform the functions envisioned for it. Creating it was like trying to construct a wholly new type of machine, from a new kind of metal, using a yet-to-be-invented welding technique.

Either of these two approaches to software is valid. The key problem is that we take on projects like #2, but pretend they are like #1. This is what ails the world of software development.

We fool ourselves about how well we understand the complex new software machines we are trying to build. Just because we plan to code a new project in a known programming language, say Java, and our engineers are good at Java, this does not mean we have answers to all the challenges that will arise in the project. Using the mechanical analogy, just because our inventors have put together many machines that use springs, gears and levers does not mean we can correctly build any machine using these parts.

We can't have it both ways. If we want an accurate budget and completion time, we cannot engage in significant research during a software project. Conversely, there is nothing wrong with research and trial-and-error, but we should not think we know when it will be finished.

But what is the solution in the real world? Everyone would like to make software engineering as predictable as traditional engineering. There are many important pending software projects with large unknowns. We cannot simply say, "Oh, this software poses some new challenges, so let's give up." The solution is to get over our hubris that software development is some special kind of animal, unlike other engineering endeavors, and that we programmers are so much smarter than our traditional engineering brethren. Software is just a machine, and people have been building machines for a very long time.

To wit, here is my prescription for improving the success rate and reputation of software developers....

• Picture each software project as a physical machine to remind yourself how complex it is.

• Be aware that in a large software project, each particular component may be understood by someone, but that is a different person for each component. No one has a grasp of the whole system, and we have no way to meld isolated individual knowledge into a collective whole. This was precisely the problem with the embarrassing tale of the Metric-English measurement error on the Mars Climate Orbiter, which wasted 300 million dollars.

- Make incremental improvements to an existing system. Sometimes this means adding a couple additional features to a working product. Sometimes it means combining two working systems with a new interface, which itself has been used elsewhere.

- Use iterative development. This applies the above principle, again and again, to one particular software system. The first release of the software does little more than say "Hello" to the user. The next release adds one basic feature. The next, one more, etc. The idea is that each software release only has one major problem to solve. If it does not work, there is one thing to fix. Each release is an incremental improvement to working software.

- In practice, of course, we may stretch a bit and include a few new features in each release, but we never attempt to create a huge, complex piece of software all at once. (See the Agile Manifesto.)

- The iterative approach also applies to time/cost estimating, with each successive estimate more accurate than the previous one.

Research projects are great, but be honest about them. The Denver Airport software disaster, cited above, could have been avoided if it were handled in this way...

1. Admit that we don't know how to sort airline baggage automatically, but would like to solve this problem.

2. Start a research project on this topic in an empty warehouse, using a few conveyor belts, some bar-coded suitcases, and some sorting gates with embedded software.

3. After working out the kinks, try the system at a small airport, for incoming flights from one other city.

4. When that works, try it for all flights to this small airport.

5. After success there, and further hardware/software refinements, create a similar system at a mid-size airport.

6. Improve the hardware/software again.

7. Install at several mid-size airports, for all flights, and fix any problems.

8. Then you are finally in a position to say, "Let's think about handling baggage at a large airport this way."

Software development need not be a mystical process, undertaken only by the most brilliant, with no hope of predicting the outcome. Software is a machine, and over many years we have learned the principles of good machine design.

Unfortunately, because software is so new and is impossible to see or touch, we get clouds in our eyes when we think about software projects. We forget that we know how to plan, design, and construct high-quality machines – by incremental improvement to previous machines, using proven materials and methods.

Resources

- AgileManifesto.org
- DreamingInCode.com
- BurjKhalifa.ae
- nytimes.com/2005/08/27/national/27denver.html (Denver Airport software)
- washingtonpost.com/wp-dyn/content/article/2006/08/17/AR2006081701485.html (FBI Virtual Case File)
- gao.gov/new.items/d06310.pdf (IRS modernization)
- en.wikibooks.org/wiki/Atlas_Shrugged/Technology (Rearden Metal)
- oig.nasa.gov/old/inspections_assessments/g-00-021.pdf (Mars Climate Orbiter failure)

What the Linux Community Needs To Grok

Foreword (January 2011)

The following essay was written 11 years ago, as the Linux operating system was starting to be taken seriously by people other than propeller-heads. Since that time, Linux has received substantial acceptance by the business and IT community as a reliable server platform. But Linux still constitutes a tiny fraction of the market for personal computer operating systems. Proof of this fact is the small number of desktops and laptops from major manufacturers with Linux pre-installed.

Why is this? Linux is certainly more user-friendly than it was in 2000. The Ubuntu distribution is quite easy to install and use, and OpenOffice is a nice application suite. Where has the Linux community fallen down in gaining wider acceptance among the general public? This is the question I addressed in 2000 in the essay below. I will leave it to the reader to decide whether my answers at that time are still true today.

After the essay is a response I wrote to the many comments that the essay generated on Slashdot.com.

Original Essay (February 2000)

Grok: to understand deeply, from *Stranger In A Strange Land* by Robert Heinlein.

Recently, I published two newspaper articles that evoked the wrath of many Linux fans. The first article was not about Linux, but mentioned it in passing. The second article was about Linux and stated the obvious conclusion that it has a way to go before it becomes the best choice for nontechnical users. The responses I received to the articles said that I was stupid, ignorant, unethical, and a pawn of Microsoft. One reader took the trouble to track down the name of my boss (at a local university where I teach part time) and wrote to him suggesting that I be fired.

I initially found this over-reaction by some members of the Linux community to be disturbing and perplexing.

Then I realized that the comments were telling me some important information about Linux, its creators and followers. Based on this experience, I believe there are a few key ideas that the Linux community needs to grok – to get clearly into its collective head.

Before stating my advice, let me make my bias clear. I hope that you (Linux developers and promoters) kick some butts in Redmond. I hope Linux and its applications become serious competitors to Microsoft's products in all computing environments for all classes of users. I hope consumers pay less for better software, and business systems become more reliable, thanks to your efforts. I agree with the U.S. Department of Justice that Microsoft engaged in predatory, anti-competitive business practices. I hope Microsoft gets their comeuppance from the Linux movement.

That said, here are the important points that the Linux community should internalize.

People set up computers alone. When people buy a new computer, they often bring the box home from the computer store, and then let it sit on the bedroom floor for several days as they screw up their courage to open it. When they do open the box, they turn on the computer fearfully and hope that it starts up correctly. If there are any problems, they have no one to call for help (other than the manufacturer's support line, which often is not very helpful).

To address this reality, new computers with pre-installed Linux should work fully and completely the first time they are turned on. When the user plugs in a standard option that they already own – printer, network, external storage device, etc. – those options should be recognized and configured automatically. For users who are installing Linux on an existing computer, the process should be nearly as simple (although perhaps more time consuming). The installation procedure should recognize and configure automatically all standard devices, adding them to the desktop or file tree as appropriate.

The model for this ease-of-setup is the Macintosh system, which truly is user-friendly. Some pre-built Linux systems and Linux installation CDs may already meet this goal. Many do not however. Some readers told me that part of the Linux installation process is to have a "Linux friend" who can edit a few files in /etc to solve nagging problems. Unfortunately, most people don't know a computer expert of any kind, much less a Linux expert. It is important for the Linux community to keep in mind that most users will be completely on their own when setting up or installing Linux systems and software.

Learning new applications is hard. Millions of people have spent years learning a particular business application suite – most likely Microsoft Office. They know the word processing keystrokes, spreadsheet menus, and graphics commands like the back of their hand. Switching to another office suite, like Sun StarOffice, is very difficult for most people. All of their existing documents, representing years of work, may import poorly to the new software. Key features that they depend on may not be present in the new application. People also are busy at their jobs. They don't have a spare 10 hours to learn the basics of some new software, or another 50 hours to get really good at it. For Linux experts, learning a new application is relatively simple. For most computer users, it is not.

Several Linux fans wrote to me stating that the "application problem" is actually a "user problem". Users are incorrectly resistant to change, the argument goes, when they should be accepting something that is new and better. This is backward thinking. People create computers to do the things that people want to do. It is not the job of the masses to adapt to your computer system. The history of business is carpeted with extinct companies that did not understand this. A good example to follow is Palm Computing, which understood what people really wanted to do with handheld devices, and captured the market as a result.

Consider focusing your immediate application efforts on the few key pieces of software that receive 90% of home and office use. Microsoft Word and America Online are near the top of this list. You might create a native Linux look-a-like for MS Word. To speed development, initially it can include just the most commonly used subset of features. Convince Steve Case to let America Online's

engineers port AOL 5.0 to Linux[2]. A Linux computer
with these two pieces of software would be a great home
system. The Wine project, if it succeeds, will provide
a longer-term solution, by allowing users to run their
familiar Windows applications "as is" on Linux.

(Note that VMware is not a solution to the application
problem. To run Windows software, VMware requires
users to load and configure three operating systems –
the virtual machine program, Linux, and Windows.
Windows applications then run on the virtual Windows
machine, not on Linux at all.)

Open source still requires good project management. The
Linux community has been on a honeymoon as it has
created the Linux software. You have been allowed to
develop the system at your own pace, put in the features
you want, and release it when it is ready. The reason for
this is that, until recently, Linux has not been mission-
critical to many important organizations. But that is
changing.

As Linux is embraced by more organizations, and used
in more ways that are crucial, the demands upon you
will increase. New feature ideas and bug reports will no
longer go onto a "wish list"; they will go onto a "hot list."
You will face pressure to add 50 new items to the next

2   January 2011 – AOL is obviously not an important application any more. But the same point still applies. What are the top
applications now for non-technical users? Does Linux run these
programs so that users don't have to re-learn new software?

release, when it really ought to have 10. Wealthy organizations, accustomed to getting their way, will demand impossible schedules from you, and then complain if the quality is not perfect.

Some readers have suggested to me that the open source method of software development causes project management issues to evaporate; that the projects manage themselves. This is a fantasy. The open source method, while it does solve some problems, raises new ones. You will be managing a large public programming project with conflicting demands, tight schedules, and the need for high quality. You have to figure out how to do this well. Hopefully, you can invent and master new techniques for software project management within the open source method. But if you don't, the complexity of this task will sink your whole endeavor.

Humility is a virtue. If Linux succeeds in a significant portion of the computer world, and it looks like it might, your time in the limelight is short.

I worked at Digital Equipment in the mid-80s, when they were on top of the computing heap. Their annual user's meeting in Boston was so large and lavish that they rented the ocean liners *Oceanic* and *Queen Elizabeth II*. DEC docked the boats next to the convention center, using them to house and entertain important customers. Executives at DEC believed they were invincible and that, if they kept doing things as they were, the good times would continue to roll. Just a couple years later, the mini-computer fad was dying and DEC failed to embrace PC's. DEC's stock sank to 10% of its previous value and before long the company ceased to exist.

Lotus nearly went out of business when it did not see that Windows was more popular than OS/2. IBM's mainframe division took a nosedive when they failed to understand the importance of mini-computers and connectivity (allowing DEC to flourish for a while).

The same thing will happen to you. The Linux killer is just around the corner. You don't know what it is, and you won't recognize it when you first see it. The next generation of techies will understand it and will consider you to be old fogies for having your heads buried in the Linux sand.

So don't get cocky. Stay humble and keep listening to your customers. If you do, you can extend your time on top for a while.

You have a chance to do something significant in the history of computing. Linux can be an important contribution that makes computers less expensive with higher quality, and causes true competition in the operating system marketplace. You can advance the state of the art in software development practice, if you can use the open source method for this large, mission-critical software system. Don't blow your chance with hubris.

Responses to Slashdot Comments (February 2000)

Thanks to everyone who posted or emailed a response. The vast majority of comments were friendly and thoughtful. I especially liked the reader who wanted to paste the article in every programmer's cubicle! More substantially, here are some specific responses to major points raised by Slashdot readers...

The Linux community is not a business, so no one can demand anything from it. This is an interesting point. You are correct in a sense. There is no "Linux phone number" for a user to call when they find a bug – even if the user is rich and important. On the other hand, there are plenty of companies that sell and service Linux distributions or systems (Compaq, IBM, Red Hat...). These companies employ Linux programmers, and have customers who want bugs fixed and new features added. Also, when the CTO of a Fortune 100 company is deciding whether to commit to Linux for 50,000 new computers, he (or she) is certainly going to be demanding. They might be a little uncertain where to direct their demands, but the overall ability of the Linux community to meet her needs is going to influence that purchase decision.

Some technical people had even more trouble than I did installing Linux. Some of the comments on Slashdot describe horror stories of smart, technically savvy people who failed in their attempts to install Linux. Or who spent 20 hours getting it to work right. Keep in mind that many future Linux users are very smart people, who happen to be busy with other things. If Linux is difficult to install or configure, these people will give up – even though they are "smart enough". They just don't have time.

My first two articles as I posted them are not exact copies of the versions that appeared in the Boston Globe. (These were the articles that evoked the flames that evoked the Grok article.) This is true, but the differences are minor. On my web site I posted the articles as I wrote them, while the Globe edited and shortened in a few places. The differences do not alter the substance or tone of either piece.

We don't want Linux used by the masses. In some ways, this is unanswerable. If someone does not want Linux to be adopted by nontechnical users (or even busy technical users), then I can't really argue with this. I suspect that many people in the Linux camp *do* want wider use of Linux however. The percentage of the population that has the skill and time to use Linux (as it currently is) is extremely small. I would guess about 0.1%. It would be a shame to limit Linux to this few. I am gratified that my article seems to have provoked a discussion on this point. What are the goals of the Linux community? Are you creating it for your use? Or wider use?

Resources

- en.wikipedia.org/wiki/Grok
- ubuntu.com
- openoffice.org
- staroffice.com
- justice.gov/atr/cases/ms_index.htm (U.S. versus Microsoft)
- winehq.org (Wine Windows emulator)
- en.wikipedia.org/wiki/ Digital_Equipment_Corporation
- en.wikipedia.org/wiki/OS/2

Do Open Source Projects Manage Themselves?

Foreword (January 2011)

The following essay was written in 2000, with the original title *Open Source Projects Manage Themselves? Dream On.* I believe that its main conclusions are still true, although some of the detailed facts about Linux and the computer industry have changed in 11 years. After the essay is a point-counterpoint about it with Eric Raymond, who has been an important advocate for open source development. He wrote a reply in 2000; I wrote a rebuttal in 2000; he added a final rebuttal this month. I appreciate Eric allowing me to include this lively exchange here.

Original Essay (September 2000)

Much has been written lately about the open source method of software development. By far, one of the most tantalizing statements about open source development is that these projects manage themselves. Gone are layers of do-nothing managers with bloated bureaucracies and interminable development schedules. In their place is a new paradigm of self-organizing software developers with no overhead and high efficiency.

The dust jacket for Eric Raymond's open source manifesto *The Cathedral and the Bazaar* makes this statement clearly. It says:

> ... *the development of the Linux operating system by a loose confederation of thousands of programmers – without central project management or control – turns on its head everything we thought we knew about software project management... It [open source] suggested a whole new way of doing business, and the possibility of unprecedented shifts in the power structures of the computer industry.*

This is not just marketing hype on a book cover, as Raymond expands the point inside:

> ...*the Linux community seemed to resemble a great babbling bazaar of differing agendas and approaches out of which a coherent and stable system could seemingly emerge only by a succession of miracles.*

Other open source adherents make similar statements in trumpeting the virtues of open source programming.

There is just one problem with the assertion that open source projects manage themselves. It is not true.

This article shows that open source projects are about as far as you can get from self-organizing. In fact, these projects use strong central control, which is crucial to their success. As evidence, I examine Raymond's fetchmail project (which is the basis of *The Cathedral and the Bazaar*) and Linus Torvalds's work with Linux. This article describes a clearer way to understand what happens on successful open source projects and suggests limits on the growth of the open source method.

(Note: This article addresses issues raised in the essay titled *The Cathedral and the Bazaar*. That essay also is included in a book by Raymond with the same title, which contains other essays as well.)

What Really Happened with fetchmail

The Cathedral and the Bazaar revolves around Raymond's experience in creating a program called fetchmail by the open source method. As he describes the software development process, he annotates the story with lessons about open source programming and how well it worked for him. One of Raymond's key points is that the normal functions of management are not needed with open source development.

Raymond lists the responsibilities of traditional software managers as: *define* goals and keep everybody pointed in the same direction, *monitor* the project and make sure details don't get skipped, *motivate* people to do boring but necessary work, *organize* the deployment of people for best productivity, and *marshal* resources needed to sustain the project over a long period of time. Raymond then states that none of these tasks are needed for open source projects. Unfortunately, the majority of *The Cathedral and the Bazaar* describes, in detail, how important these management functions are and how Raymond himself performed them.

Eric Raymond decided what piece of software he would use as a test for open source programming. He decided what features fetchmail would have, and what features it would not. He generalized and simplified its design. In other words, he *defined* the software project. Mr. Raymond guided the project over a considerable period of time, remaining a constant as volunteers came and went. In other words, he *marshaled* resources. He surely was careful about source code control and build procedures (or his releases would have been poor quality) so he *monitored* the project. And, most significantly, Raymond heaped praise on volunteers who helped him, which *motivated* those people to help some more. (In his essay, Raymond devotes considerable space to describing how he and Torvalds motivate their helpers.) In short, fetchmail made full use of traditional and effective management operations, except that Eric Raymond did all of them.

Another compelling (and often-quoted) section of *The Cathedral and the Bazaar* is the discussion about debugging. Raymond says: "Given enough eyeballs, all bugs are shallow" and "Debugging is parallelizable." These assertions simply are not true and are distortions of how the development of fetchmail proceeded.

It is true that many people, in parallel, *looked for bugs and proposed fixes.* But only one person (Raymond) actually made fixes, by incorporating the proposed changes into the official code base. Debugging (the process of fixing the program) was performed by one person, from suggestions made by many people. If Raymond had blindly applied all proposed code changes, without reading them and thinking about them, the result would have been chaos. It is a rare bug that can be fixed completely in isolation, with no effect on the rest of the program.

Lessons from Linux

In a similar way, on an even larger scale, Linus Torvalds pulled off a great feat of software engineering: he coordinated the work of thousands of people to create a high-quality operating system. But the basic method was the same one Raymond used for fetchmail. Torvalds was in charge of Linux. He made all major decisions, assigned subsystems to a few trusted people (to *organize* the work), resolved conflicts between competing ideas, and inspired his followers.

Raymond provides evidence of Torvalds' control over Linux when he describes the numbering system that Torvalds used for kernel releases. When a significant set of new features was added to the code, the release would be considered "major" and given a new even number. (For example, release 1.4 would lead to release 1.6.) When a smaller set of bug fixes was added, the release would get just a new minor number. (For example, release 1.4.8 would become 1.4.9.) But who made the decisions about when to declare a major release or what fixes were minor? Torvalds. The Linux project was (and still is) his show.

Further proof of Torvalds' key role is the fact that the development of Linux slowed to a crawl when Torvalds was distracted. The birth of his daughter and his work at Transmeta corresponded precisely with a period of slow progress for Linux. Why? The manager of Linux was busy with other things. The project could not proceed efficiently without him.

Finally, there is a quote from Torvalds himself during an interview with Bootnet.com.

> **Bootnet***: You've got a full slate of global developers who are working on Linux. Why hasn't it developed into a state of chaos?*

Torvalds: *It's a chaos that has some external constraints put on it. The only entity that can really succeed in developing Linux is the entity that is trusted to do the right thing. And as it stands right now, I'm the only person/entity that has that degree of trust.*

Open Source Revisited

So, if the open source model is not a bazaar, what is it? To the certain consternation of Raymond and other open source advocates, their bazaar is really a cathedral. The fetchmail and Linux projects were built by single, strong architects with lots of help – just like the great cathedrals of Europe. Beautiful cathedrals were guided by one person, over many years, with inexpensive help from legions of workers. Just like open source software is today. And, just as with open source software, the builders of the cathedrals were motivated by religious fervor and a divine goal. Back then, it was celebrating the glory of God, now it is toppling Bill Gates. (Some people think these goals are not so different.)

Consider three diagrams showing different ways of organizing a software development project.

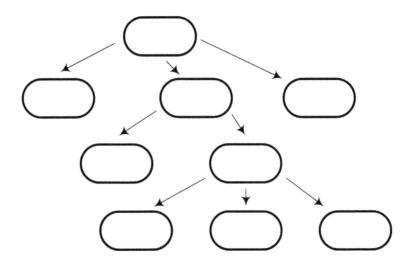

Figure 1 – Traditional Management

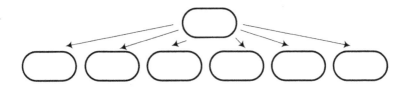

Figure 2 – Cathedral / Open Source Management

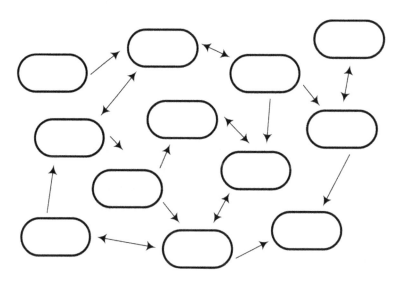

Figure 3 – Bazaar Management

The first method (traditional) shows a Vice President of Development at the top, with several Directors of Engineering reporting to the VP. Below the Directors are Engineering Managers, and finally the engineers who write the code. Many organizations use this model, and everyone agrees it is sometimes grossly inefficient.

The second method (cathedral or open source) uses a single designer/architect at the top, with many engineers reporting directly to the architect.

The third method (bazaar) is a peer-to-peer network of many engineers, all reporting to and coordinating with each other, without central control. In *The Cathedral and the Bazaar*, Raymond claims open source projects are run in the third style. In fact, they are run in the style shown by the second diagram.

For more information about the parallel between software construction and cathedral building, see the classic work of software engineering *The Mythical Man-Month* by Fred Brooks. In this book, now 25 years old, Brooks describes the chief-programmer (or surgeon) method of software development. It is remarkably similar, in its basic philosophy, to the open source method that Raymond and Torvalds used. Interestingly, the book even contains a picture of a cathedral and relates it to this style of development.

A Real Bazaar

If fetchmail and Linux were not run as bazaar projects, what would a true bazaar project look like? A real bazaar software development method would proceed as follows.

1. Someone creates a minimal working version of the software. (This follows Raymond's advice to start with a "plausible promise".)

2. The originator releases the working program, a description of how to use it, and all the source code to an appropriate forum such as a newsgroup or public web site. From this point forward, the originator becomes just another member of the user community, with no special status.

3. Anyone may download the program and source, try it out, look for bugs, and suggest fixes and enhancements. These ideas are communicated to the entire user community through the forum.

4. Anyone at any time, or multiple people at the same time, may decide to create a new version of the program. They do so by using ideas and code from the user community, along with their own contributions. They post the new version to the user forum.

5. Most likely, the code "forks" as several people create new releases at the same time. This is part of the bazaar process.

6. The user community attempts to settle on the best fork to follow, by trying all available versions and focusing their attention on the best version. No single person or small committee manages this process. Perhaps the best fork is widely recognized and quickly selected, perhaps not.

7. Several forks may live in parallel for quite a while. If so, it is the decision of the user community that no one fork is the clear winner. When the community tires of parallel forks, they will select one to follow.

8. Development continues in this dynamic, organic method. Leaders emerge briefly, as they create a new release or argue for one fork over another, but they then become equal community members again. All decisions about features, design, bug fixes, etc. are made in this way.

Would this development method work well? While I don't know this for a fact, I suspect it would not. I believe significant human endeavors (such as software projects) need some type of unified control in order to create high-quality results.

It would be an interesting experiment to run an open source project in the method I describe above. And it would be very exciting if it actually worked. This would indeed fulfill the hype on the dust jacket of *The Cathedral and the Bazaar* of a "whole new way of doing business, and the possibility of unprecedented shifts in the power structures of the computer industry."

Conclusion

I am sure many readers got out their flamethrowers at the beginning of this article, and are now resetting their weapons from *stun* to *vaporize*. So let me make myself clear. Open source projects are an important development in the computer world. The open source programming method is an exciting innovation in software engineering. But these projects do not manage themselves. They are not run by groupthink or any self-organizing dynamism. Successful open source projects are run by smart, effective project leaders. In other words, these projects have good managers.

To be fair, Raymond does address the issue of project leader control in his essay. He quickly dismisses the great importance of this control, however, by claiming that he and Torvalds did not have crucial roles in the design or creation of their software projects. He states that he and Torvalds did not design anything new, but merely recognized good ideas from others. Raymond is not seeing clearly his and Torvalds' contributions. It is very hard to shift through thousands of suggestions from swarms of users, find the good ones, synthesize them, and incorporate them into an existing code base. This constitutes strong management and central control.

The need for good management suggests the scalability of the open source method may be limited. How many people have the technical sophistication to make good software design decisions, the people skills to motivate hundreds of contributors, and the time to dedicate to a complex project? We should be wary about assuming that the open source method can solve the world's software problems. It is possible that only a small number of humans, such as Raymond and Torvalds, have the requisite skill set to run an effective open source project. If this is the case, as I suspect it is, the number of true success stories in open source development will be small. The open source method will run into the same wall as traditional software development. Good technical managers are few and far between.

Reply from Eric Raymond (September 2000)

In his article *Open Source Projects Manage Themselves? Dream On,* Chuck Connell aims some mighty rhetorical blows at a set of propositions that he believes are premises or consequences of the open-source development model. He specifically quotes, and attempts to refute, my work in *The Cathedral and the Bazaar* and subsequent papers.

Unfortunately, Mr. Connell's analysis has grave flaws. He confuses my observations about the structure of the open-source community in the large with claims about the organization of individual projects in the small. This confusion leads him up several garden paths and down a number of blind alleys.

The confusion begins immediately with Mr. Connell's title, "Open Source Projects Manage Themselves? Dream on." Of course they don't, and nobody who has ever participated in one would dream of claiming that they do. Live projects have leader/managers. In fact, most live projects have a single leader who is the final arbiter of the design. The centrality of this "benevolent dictator" role is widely understood in the community. It is so important that the community has evolved an elaborate set of customs to legitimize and regulate it; customs I have described in *Homesteading the Noosphere.*

Mr. Connell writes as if self-organization and strong central control in individual projects are incompatible, but he is crucially wrong in this. Individual projects self-organize because the participants choose to be there – they select themselves, and they choose to follow the project's benevolent dictator (or else they leave).

Above the individual project level, the community is also self-organizing. While there are projects with great prestige (such as the Linux kernel, or Perl, or Apache) which convey on their leaders wide influence, there is no manager or management hierarchy that plans for the open-source community as a whole. Instead, coordi-nation between projects happens through a horizontal trust network of relationships between individuals in a network which genuinely does look like Mr. Connell's "bazaar" diagram (his Figure #3).

Befuddled by his belief that I think leadership is unnecessary, Mr. Connell then proceeds to misread my critique of conventional management techniques. It's true that I have described some of the traditional management tasks as almost irrelevant in the Internet-centric open-source environment – notably resource marshalling, especially in its turf-war aspect. But elsewhere I refer explicitly to goal-setting and project definition as the concerns of "project leaders and tribal elders". It is not leadership that the open-source community has rejected – it is conventional management hierarchies and the pointy-haired boss.

In our world, the five functions of management that I described in CatB can only be exercised by a project lead who has credibility as a programmer and system architect. The only people who can speak for and lead the community as a whole are those who have demonstrated special competence and been elected by their peers to do so, and even they have no power to compel and must evolve a management style not dependent on being able to give orders.

Mr. Connell makes another basic error in attacking the open-source debugging process. He writes as though the most important and limiting factor in debugging is in choosing non-conflicting fixes once the problems are understood. This is wrong, as all open-source developers understand and my paper points out via a quote from Linus. In fact, the hard part is understanding the nature and etiology of each bug – and this is precisely the part that parallelizes well. Once that hard part is done, reconciling fixes is pretty easy.

By the time Mr. Connell equates our bazaar with a cathedral, his misreadings of my work and mistakes in interpreting community practice have piled up so high that he is completely out of contact with the reality open-source programmers live in every day. Thus his later claims in the article (for example about the scalability of the model) are fatally ill-founded.

It is too bad that Mr. Connell didn't acquire a better understanding of open-source development before writing this critique, because he is articulate and not stupid. His observation that individual project organization resembles a Brooksian surgical team is independent of the serious mistakes elsewhere in the article and worth followup; by coincidence, I wrote the same thing in the (not yet published) revision of CatB I'm preparing for the book's second edition.

My advice to Mr. Connell is this: spend some time in the trenches. Join a project. Observe the process in action. This paper was badly wrongheaded – but a year from now, you might have something important to contribute to the subject.

My Rebuttal (September 2000)

Background

Over the past few years, Eric Raymond has written and revised a famous essay about open source software titled *The Cathedral and the Bazaar*. This essay is popularly known as CatB. I wrote an essay titled *Open Source Projects Manage Themselves? Dream On* (MT) in which I challenged some of the basic tenets of CatB. Raymond responded to MT with the reply above (R1). Below is my continuation of our discussion.

Sample Size

In R1, Raymond writes, "[Connell] confuses my observations about the structure of the open-source community in the large with claims about the organization of individual projects in the small. This confusion leads him up several garden paths and down a number of blind alleys."

It is true that my comments in MT are based on just two open source projects, fetchmail and Linux. It is also true that I made some conjectures about the general nature of open source projects from these two cases. But this is true of CatB as well. Raymond makes many statements about the nature of open source development, based only on the same two projects. More significantly, the whole world read CatB and drew broad conclusions from it about open source programming and how to run these projects. Netscape and other companies changed their business models to match the ideas in CatB.

The moral here is that we should expand the sample size of projects we study before making firm conclusions about the base principles of open source software. (By "we" I mean everyone in the open source community and everyone interested in its outcome.)

Intention of CatB

In R1, Raymond writes, "The confusion begins immediately with Mr. Connell's title, 'Open Source Projects Manage Themselves? Dream On.' Of course they don't, and nobody who has ever participated in one would dream of claiming that they do."

It appears that Mr. Raymond has not read the dust jacket of his own book. It says, "the development of the Linux operating system by a loose confederation of thousands of programmers – without central project management or control – turns on its head everything we thought we knew about software project management." This assertion is precisely why CatB is such a famous essay. People look to the open source method as a new way to create software and, in the process, break the tyranny of Microsoft.

Now, I am pretty sure that someone in the marketing department at O'Reilly & Associates (rather than Raymond) wrote the blurb on the book's cover. But an author has a responsibility to ensure that the cover of his book basically squares with the message inside. Is Raymond claiming that the above quote on the jacket is 180 degrees opposite from the theme inside?

Organization vs. Control

In R1, Raymond states, "Mr. Connell writes as if self-organization and strong central control are incompatible, but he is crucially wrong in this. Individual projects self-organize because the participants choose to be there – they select themselves, and they choose to follow the project's benevolent dictator (or else they leave)."

Raymond has a partially valid point here. Being self-organizing and having central control are not completely incompatible – sort of. Imagine a group of random castaways marooned on a deserted island. Initially there is no hierarchy to this group. But the group may choose to elect a leader or committee to guide them. They would choose as leaders the people who seem most able to help them survive. The castaways would be self-organizing, yet have established some central control. This is analogous to an open source project that allows one member to serve as project leader, because it is in everyone's best interest.

The argument only goes so far however. Over time, leaders get stuck on certain ways of doing things and become accustomed to their power. They are resistant to change. The ability of the group to organize itself diminishes, even though it began in an egalitarian way. Similarly, open source projects are not very self-organizing two years after they start. From a newcomer's point of view, things are not as democratic as they once were.

Of course, as Raymond points out, unhappy newcomers are free to fork the project if they don't like what the leaders are doing. But this only proves that the project is no longer self-organizing – it is now two projects.

Macro Organization

In R1, Raymond writes, "Above the individual project level, the community is also self-organizing. There is no manager or management hierarchy that plans for the open-source community as a whole. Instead, coordination between projects happens through a horizontal trust network of relationships between individuals – a network which genuinely does look like Mr. Connell's 'bazaar' diagram (his figure #3)."

What Raymond says here – the lack of macro-level control over the open source community – is certainly true. This is a moot point however, since the same could be said for corporate America as a whole. No one plans the overall direction of the US economy or the computer industry. (The Federal Reserve Board does try to steer things along, but we do not live in a socialist system.)

Leaders vs. Managers

In R1, Raymond says, "It is not leadership that the open-source community has rejected – it is conventional management hierarchies and the pointy-haired boss."

No argument from me here. I have worked for many bad managers and hope not to repeat the experience. Enlightened software companies also try to find managers who are technically knowledgeable and compassionate. The open source community is not the first to rebel against bad management.

Debugging

In R1, Raymond says, "Mr. Connell makes another basic error in attacking the open-source debugging process. He writes as though the most important and limiting factor in debugging is in choosing non-conflicting fixes once the problems are understood. This is wrong, as all open-source developers understand and my paper points out via a quote from Linus. In fact, the hard part is understanding the nature and etiology of each bug – and this is precisely the part that parallelizes well. Once that hard part is done, reconciling fixes is pretty easy."

There is no question that it is a great help on any project to have hundreds of volunteers looking for bugs and suggesting fixes. The aspect of debugging that is most difficult varies with the software (and bug) at hand however. Sometimes finding the exact nature of a problem is difficult, sometimes making the fix is harder. With his many years of programming experience, Raymond must know this.

Reconciling multiple fixes also is sometimes easy and sometimes hard. It partially depends on the quality of the code. Well-designed code is simpler to fix without breaking something else. It also depends on luck. Sometimes fixes harm each other, sometimes not. Again, Raymond certainly knows this.

The Great Brooks

It R1, Raymond says, "[Connell's] observation that individual project organization resembles a Brooksian surgical team is independent of the serious mistakes elsewhere in the article and worth followup; by coincidence, I wrote the same thing in the (not yet published) revision of CatB I'm preparing for the book's second edition."

I find it fascinating that so many writers in the software engineering field keep returning to the wisdom in the *Mythical Man Month* by Fred Brooks. Sometimes I think that there was only one book ever written about software engineering, and the rest of us just keep rewriting it!

Advice

Raymond writes, "My advice to Mr. Connell is this: spend some time in the trenches. Join a project. Observe the process in action. This paper was badly wrongheaded – but a year from now, you might have something important to contribute to the subject."

My advice to Mr. Raymond: Keep a broad perspective. Don't fall too much in love with your current methods. Open source software is an important development in the computer world. So were high-level languages in the 60s, structured design in the 70s, personal computers in the 80s, and object-oriented design in the 90s. All of these movements promised to cure the ills of the software industry. (And all have helped to some extent.) Open source software is the revolution du jour of the 00s. It has pluses and minuses, just like everything else.

Raymond's Rebuttal (January 2011)

Mr. Connell writes about the open-source project ecology like a virgin theorizing about sex. His response concedes more than half of my points without grokking that they add up to something greatly different from his imaginings. I continue to think only actual experience can remedy this.

Resources

- catb.org/~esr (Eric Raymond)
- catb.org/~esr/writings/cathedral-bazaar/cathedral-bazaar/
- catb.org/~esr/writings/cathedral-bazaar/homesteading
- fetchmail.berlios.de
- torvalds-family.blogspot.com/ (Linus)
- linux.org
- cs.unc.edu/~brooks (Fred Brooks)

THE FIELD OF
SOFTWARE
ENGINEERING

Why Software Engineering Matters

I teach software engineering, and I know what "real" computer scientists think about the subject: It is soft. It is not quantitative. It is little different from sociology, since it partly concerns the behavior of people in groups.

Real computer scientists usually prefer topics such as cellular automata, undecidability, the lambda calculus, probabilistic factoring, and queuing theory. These disciplines have satisfying mathematically provable results – and sometimes an equally satisfying proof that there is no proof.

Software engineering, on the other hand, is concerned with "creating high-quality software systems in an efficient and predictable manner" – without firm definitions of what *high-quality, efficient,* and *predictable* mean. The results of the study of software engineering are heuristics for success that ought to work, most of the time, if nothing unusual happens. The methods of the field include empirical learning, policies and procedures, and people skills.

The feeling of many computer scientists toward software engineering is summed up by the following true story...

I attended graduate school in computer science after working in the software industry for several years. I signed up for the only course on software engineering and looked forward to learning some innovative programming techniques to augment my practical experience. On the first day of class, the professor introduced the course by announcing, "Software engineering is bullshit. There is nothing to teach about it. So we are going to study Unix internals instead." And that was that; the course never mentioned software engineering again. I learned nothing about the subject during four years at graduate school because the professor who taught the only course believed the topic to be empty.

While this story is anecdotal, objective proof of software engineering's second-class status within computer science can be found in computer science's most prestigious publication: *Journal of the Association of Computing*

Machinery. Over the last ten years, the JACM has published shockingly few articles about software engineering topics. (A search count at jacm.acm.org is artificially high, since it includes articles that just touch briefly on the field.)

But software engineering is not bullshit. In fact, it may be more worthy of serious study than some traditional computer science topics. Software engineering is not B.S. for the following three reasons.

- Software engineering is simply at an early stage of development.

- Software engineering happens to be hard.

- New knowledge about this subject will lead to huge gains.

Software Engineering Is at an Early Stage

In the 16th century, chemistry could barely be considered a science at all. The best statement chemistry could make about the composition of the material world was that the universe is composed of four elements: earth, air, fire, and water. But this statement had no predictive power, so it was nearly useless. Moreover, chemistry's primary goal for a long time had been to change an inexpensive substance into gold. But all the greatest minds in the world had failed to do so after

1000 years of effort. The sum of all the successes in the field was minute. At the time, we might reasonably have concluded that chemistry was a discipline not worth our time and effort. Students would wisely have been cautioned to choose another topic of study with better prospects, perhaps astrology or blood-letting.

In fact, chemistry is one of the outstanding success stories in the human search for knowledge. The success came because interested scientists persevered through lean times and because a few key discoveries opened the doors to many more.

Software engineering is in the same position. The field is young. The subject domain is vast and difficult to catalog. The goal (creating high-quality software in an efficient, predictable manner) is lofty. But new sciences always flail around with qualitative, short-lived results in their early years. The newness of a field does not mean it is less important or less worthy of our best study. The newness of software engineering, to the contrary, means it is ripe with opportunities for seminal discoveries. And with today's accelerated pace of discovery, we can expect that software engineering will take fewer years to mature than the 500 required by chemistry.

Software Engineering Is Hard

Progress in software engineering is slower than everyone connected to it would like. By progress, I mean tools and methods that consistently are helpful when creating large, complex software systems. There are many tools and methods that help in one context, but gum up the works in another. Fred Brooks has likened software development to a tar pit – where great beasts thrash violently about and quickly become entangled.

But why have other computer science topics shown relative mastery over their problem domains – analysis of algorithms and compiler design for example – while software engineering lags behind? The reason is that software engineering is more difficult.

Analysis of algorithms, compiler design, programming language semantics, complexity theory, cryptography, and other core computer science disciplines concern topics that are constrained and numerable. The problems, and acceptable solutions to them, are defined precisely. This is one of the hallmarks of these subjects. Ill-defined problems or unclear solutions are rejected as being unacceptable. Problems, or avenues of inquiry, that lead nowhere, or to vague results, are excluded from the research program. This practice of narrowing the problem statement, so the results are in an acceptable form, is practiced by many sciences and allows them to move forward.

The precision of traditional computer science has a drawback, however. The problems that are solved are those that are amenable to precise solutions. These problems are, by definition, tightly defined, with no mushy statements or an unacceptably high number of variables. In short, these problems are easier to tackle than real-world problems which are not conveniently narrowed. Software engineering happens to be a real-world problem.

The relationship between core (mathematical) computer science and software engineering is similar to the relationship between basic physics and meteorology. While the physical principles related to weather formation (heating and cooling, evaporation and condensation, air pressure) are well understood, the science of weather forecasting is far less advanced. Meteorology concerns the complex interactions of many simple phenomena. Meteorologists now can make reasonably accurate predictions about five days into the future. Forecasts beyond that are shaky. This is the case even though the individual forces that create the weather can be calculated accurately by college freshmen in Physics 101.

Software engineering is similar. In isolation, the items that make up a large software system are quite simple. The individual algorithms, file formats, and parameter passing mechanisms of a complex system are usually trivial. Mixed together by the hundreds or thousands, however, they become extremely difficult to control and their interactions are hard to predict.

The problems to be solved by software engineers are defined by the real world – creating a specific piece of software to route medical records in a specific hospital, for example. Real problems cannot be significantly simplified by artificially limiting the problem statement. We cannot limit ourselves to small medical records, or just 50 or them, or assume that the hospital network is perfect. (We might impose these limits temporarily during the software development process, but cannot allow them in the finished product.)

Software engineers face the same task as meteorologists – making sense of a vast number of interactions between simple events. Unlike weather forecasters, software engineers do have the luxury of changing some variables to cause a different outcome. (Hire more people; use a different language; get a different compiler.) This is not much comfort though, when the interactions are so complicated that we don't know what to change, or how these changes might affect the result.

None of this should be taken as a knock on traditional computer science topics. These topics are important and worthy of sustained investigation. I have spent many happy hours studying algorithms and wrote my master's thesis about them. But software engineering is a harder challenge.

The Gains Will Be Huge

The amount of time, effort, and money spent on software development and software use is immense. Software is now central to, or becoming central to, nearly everything we do – banking, medical care, public transportation, military operations, communications, education, etc. Human endeavors are impacted not just by explicit use of software (sending someone an instant message) but also by embedded software systems (stepping on a train with computerized switching, or turning on a light connected to a computer-controlled power grid).

Organizations of all sizes and types create software, often in hidden ways. Virtually every large company and organization develops software systems for internal use to help run their business. Many products, such as cell phones, that are not strictly software products contain significant software components. And, of course, companies in the software business expend all their time and effort planning, designing, and creating software.

Layered on top of the ubiquity of software is the fact that, so far, people are not very good at making it. Many studies have shown that about half of all software projects are cancelled during creation or abandoned when finished. Cost and time overruns, horrible quality, non-acceptance by users, and obsolescence before completion, are just a few of the problems that plague software development. For perspective, imagine our reaction if half of all housing starts failed or were unlivable when finished. We certainly would perceive this as a major crisis in the housing industry. This is precisely the current state of affairs for software development.

If the study of software engineering helps us improve our ability to create software, by even a small amount, the entire field justifies its existence.

Suppose some new findings in software engineering improve the efficiency or quality of worldwide software development by just 10 percent. Given the pervasiveness of software, this would have a profound economic and human impact. Even if the improvements were confined to just one type of critical software system, such as air traffic control or the Internet backbone, this also would justify all the efforts expended in the field.

In other words, software engineering matters because software matters. Software controls a significant portion of human activity, and this centrality will grow. Yet we currently do a bad job of writing software. Any gain in the efficiency, predictability, or quality with which we create software will have far-reaching effects on our lives.

The study of software engineering is not the scientific dung-heap. In fact, given the growing role of software in our world, both explicit and embedded, it is hard to think of a more worthy field of inquiry.

Software Engineering Is More than Computer Science

A few years ago, I studied algorithms and complexity. The field is wonderfully clean, with each concept clearly defined, and each result building on earlier proofs. When you learn a fact in this area, you can take it to the bank, since mathematics would have to be inconsistent to overturn what you just learned.

Even the imperfect results, such as approximation and probabilistic algorithms, have rigorous analyses about their imperfections. Other disciplines of computer science, such as network topology and cryptography also enjoy similar satisfying status.

Now I work on software engineering, and this area is maddeningly slippery. No concept is precisely defined. Results are qualified with "usually" or "in general". Today's research may, or may not, help tomorrow's work. New approaches often overturn earlier methods, with the new approaches burning brightly for a while and then falling out of fashion as their limitations emerge.

We once believed that structured programming was the answer. Then we put our faith in fourth-generation languages, then object-oriented methods, then open source, and now maybe agile processes.

But in the world of computer science, software engineering is where the rubber meets the road. Few people really care whether P equals NP. (And they are pretty sure they know the answer already.) Instead, the computer field is about *doing things* with computers. This means writing software to solve human problems, and running that software on real machines.

By the Church-Turing Thesis, all computer hardware is essentially equivalent. So while new machine architectures are cool, the real limiting challenge in computer science is the problem of creating software. We need software that can be put together in a reasonable amount of time, for a reasonable cost, that works something like its designers intended, and runs with few errors.

With this goal in mind, something has always bothered me (and many other researchers): Why can't software engineering have more rigorous results, like the other parts of computer science? To state the question another way, "How much of software design and construction can be made formal and provable?"

The answer to that question lies in the following picture.

Usability

Requirements   Maintainability

Safety
Modifiability   Portability

Testability
Design Patterns   Estimation

Scalability

Architecture Styles   Team Process

Queueing Theory
                                    Computability
OS Scheduling
                                    Algorithms
Complexity
                    Language Syntax/Semantics

Formal Specification
                                Automatic Programming

Correctness Proofs
                        Machine Learning

Network Analysis
                                    Compilers

Cryptography

The topics above the line are software engineering. The topics below the line are the core subjects of computer science.

What is that bright line that separates software engineering from formal computer science? The line can be labeled *directly involves human activity*. Software engineering (above the line) has this property, while traditional computer science (below the line) does not.

Traditional computer science has clear, formal results. For open questions in these fields, we expect that new results will also be formally stated. These topics build on each other – cryptography on complexity, and compilers on algorithms, for example. Moreover, we believe that proven results in core computer science will still be true 100 years from now. These results are never affected by human desires or frailties. If one of the researchers working in this area gets sick, or takes a vacation, the results are still true.

The results from traditional computer science might be *used* by people, but are not directly *affected* by people.

Software engineering, on the other hand, has an essential human component. Software maintainability, for example, is the ability of people to understand, find, and repair defects in a software system. The maintainability of software may be influenced by some formal notions of computer science – perhaps the cyclomatic complexity of the software's control graph. But maintainability crucially involves humans, and their ability to grasp the meaning and intention of source code. The question of whether a particular software system is highly maintainable cannot be answered just by mechanically examining the software.

The same is true for safety. Researchers have used some formal methods to learn about a software system's impact on people's health and property. But no discussion of software safety is complete without appeal to the human component of the system under examination.

Likewise for requirements engineering. We can devise all sorts of interview techniques to elicit accurate requirements from software stakeholders, and we can create various systems of notation to write down what we learn. But no amount of research in this area will change the fact that requirement gathering often involves talking to or observing people. Sometimes these people tell us the right information, and sometimes they don't. Sometimes people lie, perhaps for good reasons. Sometimes people are honestly trying to convey correct information but are unable to do so.

This picture, and the observations of it, leads to Connell's Thesis:

> *Software engineering will never be a rigorous discipline with proven results, because it involves human activity.*

This is an extra-mathematical statement about the limits of formal systems. I offer no proof for the statement, and no proof that there is no proof.

My support for this thesis is the fact that the central questions of software engineering are human concerns:

- What should this software do? (requirements, usability, safety)

- What should the software look like inside, so it is easy to fix and modify? (architecture, design, scalability, portability, extensibility)

- How long will it take to create? (estimation)

- How should we build it? (coding, testing, measurement, configuration)

- How should we organize the team to work efficiently? (management, process, documentation)

All of these problems revolve around people.

My thesis explains why software engineering is so hard and slippery. Tried-and-true methods that work for one team of programmers do not work for other teams. Exhaustive analysis of past programming projects may not produce a good estimate for the next. Revolutionary software development tools each help incrementally and then fail to live up to their grand promise. The reason is that humans are inconsistent and emotional and unpredictable.

Before turning to the implications of my assertion, I address three likely objections.

Objection: The thesis is self-fulfilling. If some area of software engineering is solved rigorously, you can just redefine *software engineering* not to include that problem.

Answer: This is somewhat true, but of limited scope. I am asserting that the range of disciplines commonly referred to as software engineering will substantially continue to defy rigorous solutions. Narrow aspects of some of the problems might succumb to a formal approach, but I claim this success will be just at the fringes of the central software engineering issues.

Objection: Statistical results in software engineering already disprove the thesis. These methods generally address the estimation problem and include Function Point Counting, COCOMO, PROBE, and others.

Answer: Despite their mathematical appearance, these methods are not proofs or formal results. The statistics are an attempt to quantify subjective human experience on past software projects, and then extrapolate from that data to future projects. This works sometimes. But the seemingly rigorous formulas in these schemes are, in effect, putting lipstick on a pig. For example, one of the formulas in COCOMO II is *PersonMonths* = *2.94* × *SizeB*, where *B* = *0.91* + *0.01* × Σ *SF*$_i$, and *SF* is a set of five subjective *scale factors* such as "development flexibility" and "team cohesion". The formula looks rigorous, but is dominated by an exponent made up of human factors.

Objection: Formal software engineering processes, such as cleanroom engineering, are gradually finding rigorous, provable methods for software development. They are, in effect, raising the bright line in the picture to subsume previously squishy software engineering topics.

Answer: It is true that researchers of formal processes are making headway on various problems. But they are guilty of the converse of the first objection: they define software development in such a narrow way that it becomes amenable to rigorous solutions. Formal methods simply gloss over any problem centered on human beings. For example, a key to formal software development methods is the creation of a rigorous, unambiguous software specification. The specification is then used to drive (and prove) the later phases of the development process. But no formal method contains an exact recipe for getting people to unambiguously state their vague notions of what software ought to do, so their intentions can be encoded in the formal semantics. In other words, a formal language for capturing requirements does not guarantee that people will use it correctly.

To the contrary of these objections, it is my claim that software engineering is essentially different from traditional, formal computer science. The former depends on people and the latter does not. This leads to Connell's Corollary:

> *We should stop trying to prove fundamental results in software engineering and accept that the significant advances in this domain will be general guidelines.*

As an example, David Parnas wrote a wonderful paper in 1972, *On The Criteria To Be Used in Decomposing Systems into Modules.* The paper describes a simple experiment Parnas performed about alternative software design strategies, one utilizing information hiding, and the other with global data visibility. He then drew some conclusions and made recommendations based on this small experiment. Nothing in the paper is proven in a rigorous way, and Parnas does not claim that everyone who follows his recommendations is guaranteed to get the same results. But the paper contains wise counsel and has been highly influential in the popularity of object-oriented language design.

Another example is the vast body of work known as CMMI from the Software Engineering Institute at Carnegie Mellon. CMMI began as a software process model and has now grown to encompass other kinds of projects as well. The software development version of CMMI is about 500 pages long – not counting primers, explainers, and training manuals – and represents more than 1000 person-years of work. It is used by many large organizations and has been credited with significant improvement in their software process and products.

But CMMI contains not a single iron-clad proven result. It is really just a set of (highly developed) suggestions for how to organize a software project, based on methods that have worked for other organizations on past projects. In fact, the SEI states that CMMI is not even a process, but rather a meta-process, with details to be filled in by each organization.

Other areas of research in this spirit include design patterns, architectural styles, refactoring based on bad smells, agile development, and data visualization. In these disciplines, some details of the work may include proven results, but the overall aims are systems that foundationally include a human component.

To be clear: Core computer science topics (below the bright line) are vital tools to any software engineer. A background in algorithms is important when designing high-performance application software. Queuing theory helps with the design of operating system kernels. Cleanroom engineering contains some methods useful in some situations. Statistical history can be helpful when planning similar projects with a similar team of people. But formalism is just a necessary, not sufficient, condition for good software engineering.

To illustrate this point, consider the fields of structural engineering and physical architecture (houses and buildings). Imagine a brilliant structural engineer who is the world's expert on building materials, stress and strain, load distributions, wind shear, earthquake forces, etc. Architects in every country keep this person on their speed-dial for every design and construction project.

Would this mythical structural engineer necessarily be good at designing the buildings he or she is analyzing? Not at all. Our structural engineer might be terrible at talking to clients, unable to design spaces that people like to inhabit, dull at imagining solutions to new problems, and boring aesthetically. Structural engineering is useful to physical architects, but is not enough for good design. Successful architecture includes creativity, vision, multi-disciplinary thinking, and humanity.

In the same way, classical computer science is helpful to software engineering, but will never be the whole story. Good software engineering also includes creativity, vision, multi-disciplinary thinking, and humanity. This observation frees software engineering researchers to spend time on what does succeed – building up a body of collected wisdom for future practitioners. We should not try to make software engineering into an extension of mathematically-based computer science. It won't work, and can distract us from useful advances waiting to be discovered.

Resources

- en.wikipedia.org/wiki/Church-Turing_thesis
- en.wikipedia.org/wiki/Function_point
- portal.acm.org/citation.cfm?doid=361598.361623 (Parnas paper)
- sei.cmu.edu/cmmi/tools/dev/

sunset.usc.edu/csse/research/COCOMOII/cocomo_main.html

A Quagmire in the Tar Pit

Fred Brooks in *The Mythical Man-Month* has described software development as similar to a prehistoric tar pit, where great and powerful beasts thrashed violently, but ultimately were unable to free themselves from death. He asserts, with obvious truth, that programming teams become mired in their own tar. The problems of software quality, limited resources, tight deadlines, and user acceptance often drag a project lower and lower until it too meets an unpleasant demise.

In an effort to tame the tar pit, various researchers in the software engineering field have proposed methods of software development that promise to bring sanity to the programming process. This is good, since software engineering certainly is a field that needs all the help it can get. But there is a problem: too many researchers have proposed too many overlapping and competing methods. The putative solutions have formed their own mess.

Sarah Sheard has described the situation as "the frameworks quagmire". She has written an article with this title that includes a frightening graphic of the overlapping, layered, and interconnecting methods.

A small portion of her picture looks like this:

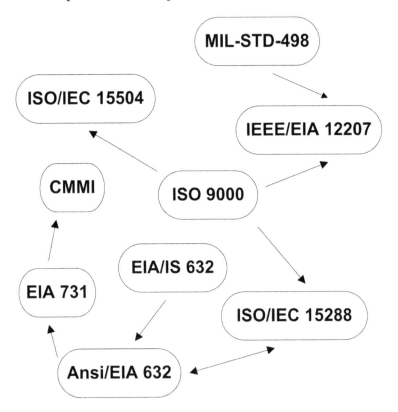

I encourage readers to see Sheard's short, valuable article for the full chart and background information. As a practical matter though, her piece is likely to leave a programming team more confused than ever, because there are several important points her work does not address sufficiently. Chief among these are:

- Why do we have this mess? Why have so many people and organizations written so many software development models?

- What should a real-life software development manager do? What standards are worth following when a manager is tackling an important, high-risk software project?

- What about the popular work of non-institutional writers such as Kent Beck (associated with extreme programming) and Steve McConnell (author of the influential books *Code Complete* and *Rapid Development*)?

There are two reasons we have so many competing software development models, one obvious and one not so obvious.

The first, and obvious, reason is the familiar "not invented here" syndrome. It is easy to think that we can create a new software development method that has all the strengths of the known techniques, with none of their weaknesses. (I have made this mistake myself.) In reality, any new framework we invent may improve current methods in some areas, but will fail in others.

The second, less obvious, reason we have so many software engineering methods vying for acceptance is that some of the competition between them is an illusion. Many of the methods operate at different levels of abstraction and, therefore, are complementary rather than competing.

An argument about whether the Capability Maturity Model for software (CMMI-DEV) is better than McConnell's books is like trying to decide whether a Chevrolet is better than a station wagon. Cars brands and car body styles are not the same thing and are not comparable. Some of the popular software development methods are actually meta-methods; they list the goals a development method should achieve, without specifying how to get there. CMMI-DEV is just such a meta-method. Other process models offer concrete prescriptions for how to run a project day-to-day. McConnell's books offer this level of detail, and can be used as an implementation plan within a meta-method.

So what is a poor software manager to do about all of this? Sheard's scary chart is no help, even though it is an accurate depiction of the frameworks quagmire. Sending your programmers to courses about dozens of competing (or overlapping) development models is not realistic. Instead, I offer the following advice for pulling your feet out of the programming tar.

Unless you are a full-time researcher in the software engineering field, don't invent another software development method! I'm sure you are a smart person, and you might even think of a few things other people have overlooked. But the world does not need another programming model right now. Rather than trying to create a better wheel, be a little boring and use methods that already exist. None of them are perfect and someday we'll have better methods, but there is probably one that fits your needs reasonably well.

Learn the basic ideas from three key programming frameworks: CMMI-DEV, agile methods, and the McConnell books cited above. These three approaches cover a heavyweight, complex management model for large software organizations (CMMI-DEV); an alternative view (agile) that can be used alone or within CMM-DEV; and an individual writer's collection of his personal tips and techniques (McConnell). If you learn a reasonable amount about these three frameworks, you will know a large percentage of the important current work in software engineering. (Note that CMMI-DEV was previously known as just CMM or SW-CMM.)

Don't be a slave to any method. Take everything the experts have written and consider it a set of suggestions that may help you. Think creatively about how the popular methods apply to your organization and your problems. Use what works and modify what does not. This advice sounds contradictory to my first tip above, but it is not. Every serious research team in software engineering knows that its method does not make sense in all situations. The method frequently criticized for being the most rigid (CMMI) actually states this caveat clearly in its opening pages. So don't place more faith in any framework than its own authors do.

By following this advice, you may be able to pull some of your paws out of the software development tar. With a little luck, your project might even flourish in the competition with the other beasts trying to beat it to the water hole.

Resources

- computer.org/portal/web/csdl/ doi/10.1109/2.933516 (Sheard article)
- amazon.com/Mythical-Man-Month-Software-Engineering-Anniversary/ dp/0201835959
- agilemanifesto.org
- sei.cmu.edu/cmmi/tools/dev/
- stevemcconnell.com/books.htm

Hey, Programmers! We Got No Theory!

There is such a thing as good software versus bad software, and there are universal principles that define good software. This is easy to see with a simple thought experiment.

I hand you two disks containing two sets of source code, A and B.

I tell you that both samples implement the same feature set, so the programs produced by A and B behave the same for all inputs. The operations performed by the programs are fairly complex, so these are large sets of source code, at least 100,000 lines each.

I tell you that A is an example of high-quality software design and implementation, while B is an example of all that can be wrong with software development.

Before you look at the source code, I ask what qualities you expect to see in A versus B.

You might answer "modularity" or "non-redundancy" or "no GOTOs". Every experienced programmer has his or her favorite list of software design DOs and DON'Ts.

If you have been programming for more than a few months, however, you will <u>not</u> say, "I have no idea. I am not aware of any general properties that lead to good software versus bad."

Experienced programmers recognize that good software looks different than bad software. Responsible programmers strive to incorporate the good qualities into their code. But our understanding of software design principles is often implicit. Good programmers seem to do a good job regularly; bad programmers always seem to miss the boat. We have little explicit knowledge about the general principles that separate the two.

The answers are important. Good design, in any medium, leads to higher quality, so a clear understanding of general software design guidelines would reduce the cost of all software development. We need *universal* design principles, so what we learn will lead to improvements across all languages and problem domains. In cases where software performs safety-critical functions, the answers impact human lives.

Despite the importance of software design, we hear little about it from software engineering researchers. We do hear a lot about software methodology – how to organize teams, manipulate schedules, and do the associated paperwork. But a process description does not tell us what design goals we are trying to achieve.

Recently, we also hear about the instantiation of design principles, i.e. patterns, both design patterns and the higher-level architectural patterns. But a pattern is not a principle. It is not explanatory. We want to know *why* a certain pattern is good and the general principles that make it effective. Examples of such principles might be information hiding, non-redundancy, and simplicity.

It is important to clarify what universal software design principles are not.

- They are not tied to a particular language or style – such as Java, object oriented design, or functional programming. There were good and bad programs written in COBOL and Fortran, long before these newer techniques came about.

- They are not related to how we create software. A team can practice extreme programming, use-case design, open source, or even CMMI Level 5, and still produce lousy software. The qualities we are looking for exist in the *structure* of the software, regardless of how some humans got the software to that state.

We currently do not have such a general theory of software design. We tackle each project separately, with few guiding principles. We follow the latest trends in software construction, with no explanation for why this year's fad is better than last year's. The issue of design principles is so important that we should be having heated arguments about it, with strong proposals, harsh criticism, and competing counter-proposals.

I published my take on software design in 2001, and that article has had considerable readership since it appeared. (See the chapter titled "Beautiful Software" in this book.) The problem, however, is not that some software teams have failed to worship the brilliant ideas in my essay. The problem is that no one is shouting it down.

If my proposal is wrong, as it may be, why is it wrong? What is the evidence for its wrongness? What would be some better ideas? What is the evidence supporting that new theory? As a community, the software engineering world is not actively searching for a universal theory of design. This is a collective failure, since progress in this direction would have dramatic impact on all software projects.

What would it look like to actively search for a theory of software design? We should emulate the worlds of physics and traditional architecture.

- We should advance theories of design, as I did in the article cited above.

- Our theories should be specific, predictive, and testable. This is a fundamental rule for science. Theories that do not make specific predictions are not falsifiable and are not part of science; they are religion.

- Competing theories are strengthened or weakened both by theoretical arguments and/or experimental evidence. The internal inconsistency of a theory might weaken it theoretically, while its parsimony might strengthen it. Experimental evidence that does not match prediction will weaken a theory (the prediction was X but in fact Y happened), while experiments that match prediction will strengthen it.

- We can use evidence both from new software projects as well as historical evidence from past projects.

All of these methods for advancing and refining theories are standard operating procedure in physics, traditional architecture, and many other disciplines. Some examples of this process within physics are string theory and the biting criticisms of it from Lee Smolin and Peter Woit. Within traditional architecture see the work of Christopher Alexander and Peter Eisenman, and their famous debate.

In most fields, some scientists typically specialize in creating theories and making predictions about the world, while other scientists specialize in designing and conducting experiments to test theories. This division of labor, while not necessary, has often been helpful. Within software engineering, we have the beginnings of this specialization, with academics on one hand, and practitioners (programmers) on the other. Unfortunately, our academics often do not look to practitioners as a source of valuable experimental data, but instead try to tell programmers what they should be doing.

Within software engineering, what would evidence supporting (or refuting) a theory look like? Suppose we believe that "information hiding" is a universal software design principle. Suppose we find a substantial software system that everyone agrees is a wonderful piece of software. It has few bugs, runs faster than its competitors, is easy to modify and scale, and is actually readable by new team members. Suppose we examine the source code and see that it violates the principle of information hiding at every opportunity. Class members are all public and are referenced throughout other classes. This program would present evidence that information hiding is not such a strong design principle after all. Or, in the least, theorists advancing the case for information hiding would have to work hard to explain this apparent counter-example.

One possibility that must be considered is that there is *no* overall theory of software design. This point-of-view holds that different problem domains (operating systems, accounting, web interfaces, etc) are so fundamentally different that there are no general principles for good design that span all domains. This is plausible. But it should be investigated in the same way as other theories. What are some example projects that provide evidence that no single principle of software design holds consistently? Are there mushy heuristics that work instead? What are they?

Another objection that might be raised to the search for software design theory is that software is not a theoretical discipline at all. Physics, and other natural sciences, seek to discover the state of the world. They want to learn about what *is*. Software development, on the other hand, tries to build something; it is more akin to mechanical engineering than biology. This is true, in a strict sense. But many areas of study that are not hard sciences look for an overall theory. This includes traditional architecture, filmmaking, industrial design, and literature. These disciplines, all concerned with making something, have long and lively histories of debate about their underlying principles. The software world seems to lurch from fad to fad without considering the nature of what we are doing and the general ideas about how to do it well.

Note that the question of how people should go about *working* on software is separate from a design theory, although there may be some intersection between the two. Apart from discovering unchanging design principles, we can separately improve the programming languages we use, the way we organize teams on a software project, the accuracy of our time/size estimates, how we test and debug, etc. A design theory would not solve all the problems of software development. But it would solve a key one.

Programmers have implicitly operated on the premise that there are no general truths about software design. Instead of starting each new project with a solid theory of design to guide us, we essentially invent our world anew each time. No wonder software development seems like a black art, and so often goes badly wrong.

What we need instead is a vigorous, active search for a small number of universal software design principles – a theory.

Afterword

While I was writing this article, the SEMAT organization began addressing some of these same questions. I looked at their work and there is considerable overlap in our basic goals. In my opinion, SEMAT can be an important contribution to software engineering research, if they can produce simple, clear results and avoid exacerbating the problem they are trying to solve. Their link is below.

Resources

- semat.org
- amazon.com/gp/product/0465092756   (*Not Even Wrong* by Peter Woit)
- amazon.com/gp/product/061891868X/ (*The Trouble With Physics* by Lee Smolin)
- patternlanguage.com/leveltwo/ca.htm (Christopher Alexander)
- eisenmanarchitects.com (Peter Eisenman)
- katarxis3.com/Alexander_Eisenman_Debate.htm (Alexander/Eisenman debate)

Index

www.ingramcontent.com/pod-product-compliance
Lightning Source LLC
Chambersburg PA
CBHW071157050326
40689CB00011B/2152